Amateur Soldiers, Global Wars

Amateur Soldiers, Global Wars

Insurgency and Modern Conflict

MICHAEL C. FOWLER

PRAEGER SECURITY INTERNATIONAL
Westport, Connecticut • London

Library of Congress Cataloging-in-Publication Data

Fowler, Michael C., 1965–
    Amateur soldiers, global wars : insurgency and modern conflict /
Michael C. Fowler.
        p. cm.
    Includes bibliographical references and index.
    ISBN 0-275-98136-3 (alk. paper)
        1. Counterinsurgency. 2. Soldiers. 3. Terrorists. 4. War.
5. Security, International. 6. Insurgency. I. Title.
    U241.F69   2005
    355.02'18—dc22   2005017475

British Library Cataloguing in Publication Data is available.

Library of Congress Catalog Card Number: 2005017475
ISBN: 0-275-98136-3

First published in 2005

Praeger Security International, 88 Post Road West, Westport, CT 06881
An imprint of Greenwood Publishing Group, Inc.
www.praeger.com

Printed in the United States of America
#60715178

∞™

The paper used in this book complies with the
Permanent Paper Standard issued by the National
Information Standards Organization (Z39.48-1984).

10   9   8   7   6   5   4   3   2   1

In Loving Memory of
Mary Janaros
1919–2004

Contents

	Preface	ix
	Acknowledgments	xiii
Chapter 1.	The Case for Global Insurgency	1
	What Is Happening?	4
	Why Insurgency?	8
	Three Factors for Success	14
	The Importance of Context	18
	The Path Ahead	23
Chapter 2.	Leadership and Mobilization	27
	Issues and Their Characteristics	35
	Organization	38
	Leadership	41
	Activation	43
	Conclusion	46
Chapter 3.	Global Insurgency Warfare	49
	Dispersal and Eclecticism	50
	Defining the Adversary	55
	Operations	57

| | | *New Battlefields* | 62 |
| | | *Warfare Redefined* | 66 |

Chapter 4.	Intelligence	69
	Direction and Planning	75
	Collection	76
	Analysis and Production	87
	Dissemination	88
	Sabotage	89
	Organized Crime	91

Chapter 5.	Funding, Procurement, and Training	93
	Funding	96
	Procurement	103
	Training	108
	Conclusion	113

Chapter 6.	A Theory of Global Insurgency	115
	Understanding Global Insurgency	115
	Frequently Asked Questions	119
	Implications	137

Chapter 7.	Al Qaeda and HMS *Dreadnought*	141
	Al Qaeda Tested	145
	Unplanned Political Agendas	148
	A New Path for Warfare	151
	What Can We Do?	155

	Notes	161
	Works Cited	171
	Works Consulted	177
	Index	179

Preface

Amateur Soldiers, Global Wars came about by an interesting route. I originally only wanted to write a paper on trends in modern conflict. I investigated intelligence, urban warfare, what wars were being fought, by whom. I found something I didn't expect, namely that these things were all being done by non-state "amateur soldiers" all over the world and not by national armed forces. It was particularly interesting in light of how much was being written about the future of warfare in its conventional form at the time. As someone who had long been interested in warfare and how it changes, this finding intrigued me. The proposed futures didn't resemble what I was seeing and reading about. These "amateur soldiers" were pulling warfare and politics in a different direction from what many experts proposed. Insurgents were turning the paradigm of modern warfare from conventional warfare to global insurgency. They were turning world politics from issues between nations to issues transcending them. This thread ran through a number of topics all of which I present in this book.

Global insurgency poses an interesting problem. The big question is can global insurgents like Al Qaeda win a war? If they can it implies that we must reorient politics and strategy to meet transnational issues as well as nations. It means we must change how we judge effectiveness in the conduct of war. If we cannot or do not find the answers to this question we cannot know if we are orienting our security correctly. We cannot know if we are hurting or helping ourselves.

As I researched and wrote, I kept a single question in mind: "How is it possible to lose many, even most battles and win a war?" Anyone looking at military history can see that it has happened but it can be difficult to understand how. An implication of this question is that the end result of force may perhaps be less important than the fact of its use. War is the servant of politics. Perhaps force must be connected directly to the political goal to be most useful in a certain context. Conversely, fighting and winning a number of battles may not be useful if the battles don't connect to the political goal. This idea is part of what makes insurgency potent and conventional war less so today. It also makes war accessible to "amateurs." It allows them to constantly keep pressure on their enemies. It allows them to survive long enough to put out their message and advance their agenda.

Some would say that insurgency even on a global level is not really war, not like World War II or the Gulf War. But if these "amateurs" can use force to achieve their political goals at a cost to their opponents, how is that not war? If war is the use of force to achieve political goals then insurgents like Al Qaeda are at war. If they are, one could say that environmental insurgents like the Earth Liberation Front are too. The same could go for other groups we have not seen yet. How is it possible to lose battles and win wars? The answer is out there, but it is ill defined. Every war is different and the way force best serves politics is a function of the politics more than the form force takes. By looking at these "amateur soldiers" and investigating the possibility of their fighting in global wars we might open ourselves to new possibilities and adapt to them.

The reader is advised that this book is a survey of the possibilities of global insurgency and not the final word on it. It is an "open source" analysis of what is going on before our eyes, purposely written with what is available to the "average human being." Yet, there is so much information to look at, weigh, and judge that it is difficult to gather it all and make it useable in a book of this scope. There are limits of resources, responsibility, and time that had to be observed. The purpose here is to call attention to the phenomenon, make the case that it exists and has implications for the future conduct of politics and its terrifying servant, war. Anyone looking for a pronouncement of how to fight and win such a conflict, or on the uses and abuses of force will not find definitive answers here. Instead, the evidence presented here is meant to convince people to ask questions and engage in debate on what war is right now and how it should be dealt with. After consulting with my publisher we agreed that this book should be made as accessible as possible to as wide an audience as possible. That is why I adopted the style this book is written in. I hope to change the minds of people about war, how it is conducted, and for what ends. I hope this book gives us all new things to think about.

It is also worthwhile to talk about what this book is not. I purposely steered away from making this a "how to book." I call attention to the possibilities regarding access to various capabilities but I have not recounted in detail how to get them or where to find them. While I am trying to make the case that this type of warfare exists and should be examined, I see no reason to assist anyone in engaging in the practice, particularly our enemies. Speaking of our enemies, the reader will also note that there is very little mention of Al Qaeda in this book until the final chapter. This is by design. This topic is broader than Al Qaeda and what it does. I am calling attention not just to them, but to groups in the future who will engage in the same things for different issues. This is a form of warfare that will be around for a long time. We need to start thinking about what it means and what we will do about it.

Acknowledgments

I have a number of people to thank for their input and support for this book. First, let me thank the people who read and gave comments: Mac Fiddner at Indiana University of Pennsylvania; Phil Melanson and Kevin Curow at University of Massachusetts, Dartmouth, and Michael Cadenazzi. Your comments and insights were great and helped me to see this topic more clearly. I also want to thank Paul Hammond and Phil Williams, former professors of mine who gave me an abundance of sage advice on both the subject matter and on how to craft a book. Thanks also to my agent, Esmond Harmsworth, for his advice and work on my behalf. I also want to thank Kim Hoag at Bytheway Publishing Services for her production services. Likewise thanks go to Heather Staines at Greenwood Publishing Group for her patience while I climbed over obstacles to this book and through my many questions for her. I want to thank my sister Maria for her help with the figure drawing and other odds and ends of this book. Finally, I must thank my parents for their love and support while I wrote this book and for being sounding boards for my ideas.

Chapter 1

THE CASE FOR GLOBAL INSURGENCY

The events of the last few years have shown that war has undergone some fundamental changes tied more to the way people think than to technological advances. These changes show up in two observable ways: a shift from conventional to unconventional war and a shift from defining combatants by land and language to defining them by issue and event. After September 11, America entered into a war against "terrorism" that will range over the entire world in a number of arenas beyond the traditional battlefield. The most fundamental difference between this war and others in history is that this one is being fought by groups and organizations unaffiliated with national governments. To fight this type of war against this type of enemy, it is necessary to gain an understanding of the way such groups are able to make war and how their actions influence current ideas on the conduct of war.

This is an exploration of what people are doing and how they are changing warfare by engaging in new practices. These practices are not always a conscious effort to change war, but the potential is there for a new model of warfare involving amateur soldiers, the things they do, and what makes it all possible. Within this framework, a discussion takes place on what makes these practices possible.

Since the fall of communism, much has changed socially, politically, economically, and technologically. We went from a time when access to travel, technology, communications, and the production of wealth was limited by national governments to the current time when that access is wide open to many who want it. Yet, this exploration is not about technology. It is not about networks or telecommunications or smart weapons. They dominate television documentaries and print media because they are interesting to watch. Technological innovations play their part and are relevant, but they are tools to carry out action. They only work when used correctly. They only produce results when part of a good strategy. They only grant success when helping to achieve political goals, and that never changes in any age with any tools.

War is now accessible to many more people outside professional military circles, as seen on September 11. Other people will develop operations of their own. They will have a unique imprint that comes from people who acknowledge no rules of war and regularly break with conventional wisdom. That is the point of this investigation. People, nonprofessional, unaffiliated people, are engaging in warfare in the form of civil wars, guerrilla wars, and private conflicts. In ages past, going to war was normally the province of governments and their professional armed forces, and they alone fought. Now, not only is it possible for nongovernmental, nonprofessional armies to fight, but also it is possible for them to do it globally in a way that most national armed forces cannot. Before, war was conventionalized; now popular access has expanded to support politics, and the machinery of war has expanded to unconventionalize modern conflict as the people involved make their own rules. This differs from past insurgencies in that the politics is transnational, and the scope of operations is global.

The idea of global insurgency is important not as a new form of warfare but for what it implies. If war is the servant of politics, then making war accessible to popular movements allows those movements to advance political agendas outside national governments or in actual opposition to the political agendas of national governments. This opens the world to a good deal more change for good or ill; it will mean chaos rather than order in the post-Communist age.

Because this is a fledgling attempt to isolate and describe a new phenomenon, there will be holes in the picture. We can take what we observe and try to explain what it means and how it works. It will help us understand the future. It sounds theoretical, and it is. But, if it is done right, a good theory helps us understand what is happening, what will happen, and why. Although there is a good deal of theory behind this topic, make no mistake: It is real. Real actions are being taken, and real blood is being shed in the name of real political goals. In light of September 11, we must be aware of these possibilities.

Finding the right terminology to describe this phenomenon has been challenging. Groups unaffiliated with governments are engaging in war writ large. Global insurgent war with tools approximating what governments use to contend with them worldwide is new. But, fixing a label to that does not always work out well. Labels are attempts at finding the boundaries of what something is and is not. Any sort of group can do the things this book discusses, so boundaries do not serve the discussion of what is happening.

The term nongovernmental organization (NGO) could have been used, and many groups involved in this type of conflict could be considered NGOs, but not all of them would. The problem with using NGO as a term is that it lumps the peaceful groups and the potentially violent groups together and masks other groups. NGOs should be included, but they are not the only groups that could be engaged in these activities. Likewise, one could use terror groups. Again, many other types of organizations could be included in this discussion also, and the term terror groups obscures these other groups that might take part. Some organizations could be militia or issue-oriented organizations ranging from the peaceful to the violent. Other iterations of terms included subgovernmental organizations, subgovernmental agents, and extragovernmental agents, extragovernmental organizations. None of these terms offer the freedom or inclusiveness the subject seems to need. This inclusiveness is necessary because no rules govern who does this. Anyone, any time, and in various roles can be involved in this type of war, so definitions must be included that can cover all of the potential participants.

We can classify these groups by their characteristics. They are issue centered. They are activist organizations capable of servicing an agenda that transcends governments or multilateral organizations. They are not always officially registered anywhere. They are not always violent. Actually, it is better in classifying these groups to say simply only government and government-related groups are excluded from this definition.

So, what label can we use? The terms this book uses are issue organizations, issue groups, and issue constellations. *Issue organizations* can be any type of organization advancing an issue or agenda through an action. More than one organization together is an *issue group*. A grouping of organizations representing different but related issues is an *issue constellation* (more explanation is given in Chapter 2). The terminology is purposely being kept simple in the hopes that, as more evidence becomes available, it will generate debate that will yield better discussions and better results. It is not necessary to search for buzzwords to revolutionize the study of warfare. Instead, we simply call attention to the beginning of what will be an important phenomenon. Terms were needed to encompass the subject, and the existing ones did not fit, hence the use of issue organizations, issue groups, and issue constellations.

What Is Happening?

Governments fight issue organizations or groups more than they fight other governments currently. Since 1989 when communism fell, only a handful of conflicts have actually occurred between governments. The Gulf War was a traditional conflict between nations, as has been the continuing conflict between India and Pakistan over Kashmir (although many insurgent factions on both sides seem to take part). Most of the other conflicts were fought, on one or both sides, by issue organizations/groups. This has happened without fanfare, which is surprising because it is both widespread and deviates from history. Insurgents have attempted to break away from national governments in Chiapas, Mexico, Chechnya, Russia, and Sri Lanka, among other places. Global insurgencies like Al Qaeda have staged a variety of operations aimed at destroying Western people and holdings of various types all over the world. They have been very active in ways that are in many cases shocking. However, little has been said about the changes they bring to warfare until now.

Issue organizations/groups take many forms but can be characterized in this way. They are unaffiliated organizations trying to advance an issue not addressed or supported by a government. The issues are either considered beneath the notice or beyond the scope of national governments. The organizations can be benign, like human rights organizations, or violent, like the Tamil Tigers of Sri Lanka. Issue organizations/groups have existed for years in various forms. What gives them power now is the state of the world today. Several things, some technological and others philosophical, have come together at this point in time to allow issue organizations/groups power they did not previously have. Modern communications allow organizations of like mind on a given issue to band together into an entity potentially as powerful as a government. The fall of communism opened the world political system for a number and variety of issues to take form and gain substance. Private concerns could gain access to more resources and attract more people to their cause. This means that issue organizations/groups are able not only to advance their agenda, but also could use violence to make it happen.

One may well ask how an issue organization/group engaging in violence is different from terrorism. There has been a good deal of debate on the definition of terrorism. That debate and the term itself obscure investigation of the use of global insurgency warfare by issue organizations/groups. The actions commonly associated with terrorism (aside from September 11) are actions that have been taken by combatants in many wars throughout recorded time. Calling the acts terrorism (a relatively recent development) is a device to delegitimize the actions and their associated political goals. Terrorism is a term directed by one side to delegitimize political violence by its opponents (which national governments claim a monopoly on); it is criminal activity. Allowing the violence to become known as something else (e.g., rebellion, civil war, or interstate war) gives the violence a legitimacy that many governments are unwilling to surrender. In giving the violence legitimacy, the cause behind the violence is also given legitimacy. These are valid legal and political considerations, but they tend to obscure the investigation of how issue organizations/groups can conduct war. Because the term and the debate do not lend to an understanding of global insurgent warfare, it will not be used.

Political violence, regardless of its source, regardless of whether it has any legitimacy, must be answered. The answer, even if the tool used is political violence, must aim at defeating the issue causing the violence. Calling it criminal activity implies that arresting the perpetrators settles things, even if the issue that precipitated the violence remains. Because issue organizations/groups tend to be issue oriented, it seems less than useful or unrealistic to dismiss them as terrorists. The terrorism debate hinders an understanding of the nature of issue organizations/groups and the way they make war.

Issue organizations/groups are having success in fighting governments by using insurgency to subtract advantages from their opponents rather than overpowering them. After the Gulf War, it became apparent to anyone watching that there was no longer a future in fighting conventional armies in conventional wars on conventional battlefields. This not only applies to nations like the United States, but also to any nation that can afford to field an army equipped with modern weaponry and training. Such a nation can be quite successful on the conventional battlefield. For issue organizations/groups, it becomes more difficult to do this if they intend to oppose national armed forces because they not only need resources and military hardware but also safe areas in which to assemble and train an army. Doing so would make them a target easily destroyed by their enemies. Instead, they have learned to operate in ways that level the field and force others to fight without the advantages on which they have come to rely.

There are examples today that give glimpses of the possibilities of war in this fashion. They are happening all over the world. Probably the most salient examples visible to the average human are the global and violent actions of Al Qaeda. But, there will be other examples besides Al Qaeda. Global insurgents are changing warfare by pulling it away from high-tech weapons on the battlefields to suicide bombing and ambush in urban settings. Organizations are gathering millions of dollars to assert an agenda and using that money to purchase weapons and equipment on either the open or the illegal market. All of the examples reinforce the idea that warfare is changing, and not all of the changes are offered by professional militaries.

Al Qaeda seems to be able to generate violence anywhere in the world. That is exactly the idea its leadership wants to portray to the world at large for its own constituencies, for its enemies, for all who have not chosen a side. Its actions reinforce its power to members, give cause for fear to its enemies, and convert new members to its cause.

There are many national armed forces around the world that cannot strike globally. Indeed, the nations that can project force globally comprise a small list and include America, Britain, France, Russia, China, and India. Al Qaeda has proven that they also can. This is something to keep in mind in reading this book as it hints at the power of this type of war. Nations that cannot project power internalize, and their agendas rarely transcend borders. Al Qaeda does project power abroad, and that allows it to export its political agenda as well.

Al Qaeda has bombed the World Trade Center and taken responsibility for bombings in Egypt, Indonesia, and Pakistan as well as the Middle East. They may be the first group engaging in this type of war. The war in Chechnya is another example. The Chechens are attempting to gain their independence from Russia through force. To that end, they have exported their violence quite far from Chechnya. The hostage situation at a Moscow opera house in the fall of 2002 illustrates that they can strike Moscow if they choose, even from nearly a thousand miles away.

These organizations are also able to gather funding, put out their messages to the media, and recruit new members to continue their fight very much like national governments do. The U.S. government is expending a good deal of effort to track Al Qaeda funding sources, of which there are many.

We can note also the rise of transnational criminal organizations. In and of themselves, they bear many of the marks of these other organizations except that they are not advancing political agendas, although they possess capabilities that could be harnessed in support of such organizations. These capabilities include funding, weapons trafficking, intelligence, and espionage. Because these criminal organizations are global, they can engage in espionage worldwide. The weapons in which they traffic can range from small arms to materials for weapons of mass disruption.

The situation becomes one in which most nations of the world cannot compete with organizations that can go out and buy what they want rather than go through research and development processes.

These organizations gather money for their operations, but they do not have to provide services like health care, electricity, or sanitation for their members the way governments must for their citizens. This frees the money to be used for operations rather than member welfare. Ironically, members are citizens of nations and live off of those services instead.

There are other examples to consider. Note the various global protests taking place. The protests in Seattle, Washington, against the World Trade Organization summit in 1999 brought together a number and variety of organizations. These organizations showed solidarity with each other on that one issue in Seattle when in other instances they might never come into contact. All of this is in the name of one basic issue in which these organizations have a stake and want to take action. The fact that they were able to bring thousands of people to bear on Seattle is and should be ominous to analysts for the potential it represents. If thousands or tens of thousands of people can be convened in a city for an issue and they can stop traffic and engage in acts of civil disobedience or disorderly conduct, then they can also convene in a city with weapons.

Examine the protests against the Iraq War in February 2003. Look at those protests and note the sheer numbers of people taking part, in many cases thousands of people, approaching 1 million in some locations. They all protested on the same day in concert. They were all protesting one issue. There are a number of things they could have done besides protest. What if all those protesters convened some day in various cities to do violence? Are not 50,000 people armed and violent capable of taking over city, at least in the short term?

This ability to convene people is in some portion caused by modern communications. However, people banding together to fight is not a new phenomenon. Information technology enhances the ability and the desire to band together; it does not create those things. People have been banding together to advance causes for centuries. Indeed, when the Romans colonized northern Europe, they were faced with many tribes that wanted the Romans to leave but did not associate with each other. To oust the Romans, they attempted to unify. The Romans opposed this, starting a conflict highlighted by Roman attempts to divide and rule northern Europe and tribal attempts to unify and drive out the Roman presence. Ultimately, the draw to be independent outweighed other considerations, and Rome was defeated and sacked by one of these tribes.

In microcosm, we can look at the U.N. intervention in Somalia in 1993. The incident in which U.S. Army Rangers attempted to take the warlord General Aidid into custody illustrates the convening of numbers of people in a city to do violence. When the Rangers attempted to seize General Aidid, he was able to mobilize a number of armed fighters quickly to the spot where the Americans were and engage them in a firefight described in the book *Blackhawk Down*. They failed because of the discipline, training, and firepower the Americans were able to bring to bear in their own defense. However, the fact that so many Somali fighters were able to take part in that battle (perhaps more than 1,000 Somali casualties) should illustrate to all that people can be mobilized relatively quickly and easily to fight. It happened in Somalia, and it can happen on a much larger scale in other places.

For other examples, we can look at the character and places of political violence. Where once national armies dueled each other on battlefields in head-to-head confrontations, conflict since the Gulf War has taken on a far different cast. Now, the violence is ambush, assassination, and suicide bombing, and the counter moves to these actions. Large-scale military operations have been replaced by smaller-scale operations to defeat this violence.

Likewise, battles no longer take place in large open spaces outside cities such as with D Day, the Battle of the Bulge, Waterloo, and many others throughout history. Now, fighting has taken place inside cities like the city of Grozny in Chechnya, in Mogadishu, and in a number of cities in the Middle East. This tends to limit the usefulness of precision-guided weapons and many other technologies and tactics that work well in large open fields but not in the confines of congested city streets, which, as it happens, are perfect places for ambush and suicide bombing.

That these organizations are engaging in conflict is important. The fact that they are shaping the way war is fought is more important. Look back over the years since the Gulf War. For all of the political violence that has occurred, little has been nation against nation. Most of the violence has been fought by issue organizations/groups, and if it seems to some that this sort of violence is terrorism and not war, let the following case be made. It is widely accepted that war is violence aimed at fulfilling political goals. If the so-called terrorist acts successfully fulfill political goals, even if those goals are not national goals, is that not war? If national armies are brought to take action to respond to it, are they not engaging in war? This makes the case for the importance of amateur soldiers engaged in global wars.

Why Insurgency?

Because cities are congested, it is difficult for national armed forces to use the type of long-range precision-guided weapons seen in the

Gulf War against insurgents. This means that fighting must be done up close by soldiers with small arms and light artillery. The combination of not being able to use the most effective weaponry in a city and fighting an enemy indistinguishable from the civilian population strips away important advantages to modern weaponry: the ability to spot the enemy early and destroy them at long ranges.

Issue organizations/groups assemble and move much quicker than conventional forces and government bureaucracies. It took the Allied armed forces nearly 6 months to assemble the forces they needed to invade Iraq in 1991. By any standard, that is a long time to prepare to take action, but it was necessary because the types of weaponry used (tanks, ships, planes) needed to be transported, as did their crews and supplies. They needed to be prepared for operation in a desert environment. Failure to take this time to prepare could have resulted in disaster for the Allies in the Arabian Desert. Insurgents do not seem to need the same time to prepare. Because they mainly use small arms and light-crewed weapons or high explosives, they can move quickly and disappear quickly as the need arises. Thus, in a case like the American expedition in Somalia in 1993, General Aidid was able to assemble hundreds (or more) of his soldiers quickly to attack the U.N. forces in Mogadishu in a relatively short time. Many insurgent issue organizations/groups also have what is often called a "flat organization"; that is, there are fewer layers of bureaucracy between the decision makers at the top and the soldiers on the bottom. Orders can be passed quickly, and actions can be taken quickly.

Insurgent forces have less dependence on specialized supply. As noted, they do not use tanks, planes, or ships. As a result, they do not require large amounts of specialized fuel or specific types of ammunition to fight. Much of what they need (food, water, bullets, cell phones) can be carried by the individual fighter. It can be hidden, even in large quantities, in unobtrusive but easily accessible places like houses, garages, and the like. It can be smuggled anywhere. It is produced in large quantities and can be gotten without the lead time needed to produce more. It is cheap, so more can be obtained for less money than the hardware used by national armed forces.

Insurgents in issue organizations/groups have better local knowledge of their operating area than their opponents. Because of their dispersed nature, these insurgents often live in the areas in which they operate, as insurgents have in days past. As a result, they become very familiar with the areas where they operate and know the people with whom they live, how to navigate the area, where to find things they need, and who will help them, when, and for what. When faced with conventional armed forces, especially expeditionary forces from other countries, this becomes a coveted advantage. Particularly when fighting in cities, local knowledge means the difference between being lost and knowing how to get where you want to go. It is the difference between setting an ambush and being ambushed. It is the difference between being caught by your enemies and escaping from them to fight another day.

Another advantage insurgents have is camouflage. Since the beginning of time, armies have fought each other using devices of some kind (uniforms, flags, etc.) that established who was on what side. Knowing this made it easier to control the battle or at least know who was winning. Conventional battles also tended to be fought at sea or in fields away from the civilian population. It was easier to maneuver in the open, and doing so avoided severely damaging the assets that were the subject of the fight. But, the insurgents tend to be living among civilians; in many cases, they also are civilians. They dress as civilians and live with them. This makes them difficult to distinguish from civilians for terms of fighting wars. Because in most cases government armies wish to avoid unnecessary destruction, this presents a problem in prosecuting wars with issue organizations/groups. It precludes the use of more effective weaponry that may have collateral casualties among noncombatants. Ruling out indiscriminate force also rules out large-scale operations in favor of smaller units and operations that often take more time. Indeed, because the combatants and noncombatants are indistinguishable, the use of indiscriminate weaponry is moot in any war in which the hearts and minds of the noncombatants are part of the stakes in the fight.

Insurgents tend to use the standard operating procedures (SOPs) of their opponents against them. Conventional armed forces rely on SOPs to train large numbers of soldiers in the preferred way of doing things. All soldiers operate with the same understanding, and this allows for the coordination of those soldiers in a way that is necessary to fight conventional wars. Part of the outcome of SOPs is that they establish a predictable pattern of behavior for those who are trained in it. Someone who knows the SOP can make people trained in that particular SOP behave in predictable ways, using that as a weakness rather than a strength. This is particularly true if the SOP is weak or only partially practiced. An observer can then note the weaknesses in the SOP to wreak havoc in unexpected ways.

Many governments inadvertently reinforce these conventional warfare weaknesses. Many, but not all, still plan to fight against peers, not insurgents. Governments tend to defend against threats to power. For some governments, the threat is internal, and they prepare to fight to keep power from slipping away to rival factions such as issue organizations/groups. But for many governments, the threat to their power is from a neighboring country or a rival for regional influence. As a result, they tend to orient to deal with threats from peers. Again, acknowledging a rival is difficult for a government because there is an implicit acknowledgment that the rival offers a competing model of how to live that people might follow. Moving beyond that, it is easier for governments to fight well-defined peers with a well-defined composition and power than to combat something ill defined in a war with no clear end. It is easier to field a budget and justify it to a legislature. It is easier to explain the war to people and convince them to fight. It is always easier to conduct an "us-versus-them" war. It is much harder to fight that war when some of them are among us.

In the wake of the September 11 attacks, the U.S. government is centering its efforts on Afghanistan and Iraq and not the network of worldwide insurgents responsible for the attacks on New York and Washington. This should not surprise anyone. It is well known that a headquarters for Al Qaeda (the organization held responsible for the attacks) was located in Afghanistan. Yet, as the Taliban falls to its American-backed rivals, it is unclear what damage has been taken by the organizations responsible for this attack, earlier attacks, or future attacks. It is also unclear what should be done after the fall of the Taliban because all of the other governments on Earth outwardly deplore the September 11 attacks and support America to varying degrees on that issue.

Iraq was the next nation to feel American wrath because they were believed to possess weapons of mass destruction and had shown a willingness to use them. This seems to reinforce the model of governments punishing other governments as a reaction to "terrorist" violence, even though the organizations responsible clearly are scattered worldwide (including in America). It is perhaps hoped that in punishing governments from which these organizations obtain support, they can extinguish the people responsible. This is unfortunate in that it also tends to propel new recruits to these organizations and buys them more support. In particular, because the organizations are not specifically damaged, they are willing to see others take such damage to further their cause.

It is much easier to visualize taking land or cities, bombing targets, or destroying armed forces of other governments. These are concrete things that measure traditional success. It is easier to report to the people and the media that a city has been taken or a battle has been won to keep spirits up and keep support of all types feeding the effort. They are reassuring to people and decision makers alike. For insurgents, the fall of a sanctuary simply heralds the opening of a new one somewhere else but with the same agenda. The bombing of a training facility is a temporary condition as long as the trainers and their knowledge still exist. A way must be found to combat the issue organizations/groups where they live and disrupt the way they work. The first place to start is by investigating the issues driving the issue organization/group and the agents it employs to gain its ends.

It is hard to visualize going to war against an issue and its agents. In particular, it is nonquantifiable. Yet, this also is politics by other means (to paraphrase Clausewitz).[1] If war is the servant of politics, then the type of war used serves a political issue, as all wars should. In a war against an entity with multiple parts of indeterminate authority, with whom do you negotiate? In a war in which the enemy is scattered and hidden all over the world, where do you go to seek them? How do you measure the effectiveness of the strategy: body count, seizure of resources, public opinion polls?

There is no clear way to see an end to this type of war or how long it will take to prosecute because it does not really resemble other wars. There is no readily apparent historical example on which to build a model. Yet, the task of changing frames of reference to meet this type of war cannot be impossible. The criteria must change. Fighting global insurgency will probably entail more qualitative measures of effectiveness than quantitative measures. Insurgents do not seem to fight a war of numbers. They fight a war based on philosophy, ideals, and thought processes (another way in which they level the playing field with governments).

Global insurgents fight more often and with less restraint than government forces. Again, there are two different entities operating in two different political atmospheres. Aside from anomalies like the Nazis, governments must show restraint in the use of the armed forces. They are costly, and winning a war is sometimes as costly as losing one. Insurgents seem to care less about costs. Their fighters can go wherever there is a war and fight. If the fight is lost, it does not mean the end of the issue organization/group. Because they are not beholden to the conventions for fighting wars to which nations adhere, they can be particularly daring or particularly brutal.

Insurgents learn to use imagination and nontraditional means to attack nontraditional as well as traditional targets. This was made plain to the whole world on September 11, 2001. If wars were only made by governments, the destruction of the Pentagon or the World Trade Towers would have called to mind incoming missiles flying to their targets, skies filled with planes, or ships at sea engaged in pitched battle. Instead, the image was of hijacked passenger liners being driven into those buildings in broad daylight with no warning and no battle of any kind. The attack was shocking, audacious, unprecedented, and devastatingly effective.

No one should see this attack as a fluke or an isolated incident. The history of unconventional warfare is filled with shocking acts like this, although not on this scale. Such use of imagination is what the "weak" use in battle with the strong. If an opponent cannot be overpowered, they can be unbalanced by quick imaginative action in a way and in a place the opponent does not expect. Blitzkrieg, Pearl Harbor, the Tet Offensive, and the September 11 attacks all followed this pattern.

Issue organizations/groups learn to fight few conventional pitched battles and have less formality to their actions. It would be suicidal for an insurgent force, armed without tanks, planes, and ships, to seek a conventional battle with conventional forces. In fact, because they do not seek traditional war goals like territory or national power, there is no reason to seek decisive battle. This is a change from unconventional warfare as Mao knew it, for instance. Mao wrote that ultimately the unconventional force must become a conventional force to defeat and overthrow the government and take political power.[2] That was his goal in China. Issue organizations/groups, on the other hand, do not seem to seek national power. Their motivations transcend national issues in many cases. So, it is never necessary for them to form a conventional army. Instead, they fight when the opportunity to inflict damage on weakness presents itself and helps to achieve political goals.

Global insurgents fight in a way that directly links their actions to their political goals. That is, they plan their operations in such a way that mere execution of the action achieves some form of the political goal. If the act is successful, the goal is achieved that much more forcefully. One can note that the September 11 attacks entailed the hijacking of four planes and their subsequent collisions with the Pentagon and the World Trade Center. The targets chosen represented American military and economic power. The attacks were designed, by destroying the symbols of American power, both to disrupt the economy and defense of the nation and to deliver a message that even America is not safe.

But, it should not be lost on anyone that even if the four planes had been hijacked and all simply crashed into the ground without hitting their targets, the attacks would have been considered successful in demonstrating that America is not safe and disrupting the economy and security of the nation. Even if four attempts at hijacking had been made and only one or none was successful, the same message would have been registered. The fact that the attackers were so successful simply makes them look that much more fearsome and gives that much more weight to their political agenda. This is the

chief strength of unconventional warfare, and it needs further investigation both to conduct it and to combat it.

Three Factors for Success

Why is it that unconventional warfare seems to be so successful? It
is not an innately superior form of warfare. In the preceding section, it
was noted that Mao (a renowned insurgent) held that unconventional
forces cannot win a war unless they are in concert with or become
conventional forces. But, in limited wars that have goals other than
the taking of national power by one side over the other, a good deal of
flexibility is involved. Then, an unconventional force can plan to take
actions that are aimed directly at achieving the political goals in a way
that conventional forces do not. This gives unconventional forces a
large advantage in wars they fight. Because operations can be geared
directly to political goals, the planning of operations takes on a different cast from warfare between conventional forces. Global insurgents
have four types of advantage over governmental forces: context, organization, adaptability, and creativity.

The key, the thing that makes these global guerrilla actions possible, is access. Access (to weapons, to communications, to people) allows the changes we see to happen. Anything can be a key to change,
and it is not always clear which factors are key in any given time.
Technology, ideas, politics, or combinations of these things could be
the key to change. But, for change to happen, that is, the kind of
change discussed here, the key is access. It allows action beyond the
control of those with a vested interest in opposing change. Those who
oppose change will attempt to gather everything they can to ensure
the survival of the status quo. Now, their opponents can do likewise.

For those who want change, everything begins and ends with access to the means to change things. This dynamic has driven many of
the newsworthy political events of the last 10 years. That people want
to change things is not new. The fact that people have access to the
means to change things is new. To gain access, a device is needed,
something that opens the door that grants the access. The point here
is not about tools. Often enough, changes in the world since communism's fall are ascribed to the tools (information technology,
precision weaponry, etc). The tools are not the point; the role they
played in providing people with access to political power is the point.

Think of it this way: Decide you want to go to the moon. People
have wanted to go for ages, perhaps since early humans first beheld a
full moon in the evening sky, wondering if they could get there from

here and wondering what they would find if they could. Until access to the technology became available, going to the moon was a dream. The technology became available to make it possible, but it only became a reality when political power backed it and moved forward with the effort. When building a rocket so you can go to the moon, the rocket seems like the access device, but the technology only works when coupled with the political mobilization that provides money, people, and material focused on the idea.

The building of the atomic bomb is a related example. To build an atomic bomb, certain things are needed. Some of these things are technology driven. The first thing that was needed was the overall idea that splitting the atom would create fantastic energy release, and that human hands could re-create that chain reaction. Once that was done, the technology was developed (another part of the device). Finally, the political backing of a government was necessary to provide finance and resources (a final part of the key). But, the featured part of the device was the idea. Without that, the technology would simply have been used for other things, and the political will would have focused on something else.

The lesson of these examples is that for any sort of human endeavor, access to power is the key. Whether going to the moon, building an atomic bomb, or changing the world, no one can accomplish anything unless either someone with power is willing to let that happen or people have the ability to make things happen themselves. It is the latter that is happening right now. Regular people have the access to the things that allow them to change the world even if national governments are either indifferent or opposed to those changes.

Here is another, more modern example. Dream of making the world to your own liking, the way you want it to be. We all do it, but we set those dreams aside because we have lived knowing we do not have the capabilities at our disposal to make such changes—at least not until now. Before, we could all visualize how we wanted the world to look, but that vision could only go forward with the support of a government. The only machinery available for change was governmental; if government granted access, changes could be made, and if not, the status quo remained. This meant people either had to be content with the status quo or had to take control of governmental power to make changes, in which case those people would be branded outlaws and be faced with death or in rare cases succeed in the overthrow of a government. This is where the idea that "you can't fight City Hall" comes from.

Why can't you fight City Hall? City Hall sets the agendas and mobilizes the capabilities to grant the agendas. Implicit in its existence is the vested authority to do those things. This means City Hall can do as it sees fit in selecting and executing goals. City Hall decides which agendas it will advance, which it will ignore, and which it will oppose. With that authority, whether through social contract or military force, they can mobilize all of the capabilities available to them. In the light of that, it has been the lot of the masses to go along with government agendas and support them wholeheartedly or oppose them if they can.

Here is where the changes are manifested. Where once change came through governmental indulgence or civil war, now change can come without governmental machinery. People, ordinary people, can effect political change. They can make a world to their liking, forming their own community and taking action. They may be a minority in the nation they live in, and no one there may be receptive to change, but inevitably like-minded people exist in other places, and it is now possible to band them together and take action. They can build their own services to meet their agenda. They have access to things that allow them to form duplicate services to those governments used to go to war.

Making the world over can be done without governmental support, with smaller goals and a smaller agenda. The makeover can be subtle or blunt. Best of all, they can be done without seizing the governmental apparatus. This means a civil war does not have to take place before the agenda can be adopted and executed. Political change will still be violent, but now it can occur without revolution; that is, the change can be activated by anyone, at any time, without warning. Once the goals have been achieved, the issue organization/group could then disband or move on. Permanence is not in all cases a requirement for this kind of war.

The case can be made that broad humanity now has greater access to everything than ever before to change their political environment and the way they live. It is worthwhile to discuss in more detail access and its influence on the rise of global insurgency. The access is the result of combinations of factors that permeate the world right now. There are three conditions to consider: the openness of the world political and economic system after the fall of communism, availability of technology, and the free flow of ideas across borders and around the world.

The open world political system is a reaction to decades of cold war. During the cold war, half of the world was closed off to the other half. This meant things like investment and economic growth were not widely available everywhere. There was no mechanism for the free flow of goods and services or ideas between Communist and capitalist worlds. Politically, each side mistrusted the other. Each side was wary of the possibility of corruption by the other. The closed society also feared Western solutions to problems that would have lessened the near-total control of the Communist Party. The world political system was closed and allowed little change.

Then, without firing a shot, communism fell. When that happened, people all over the world began to see the restrictions to world politics and economics fall away. The world became wide open to investment and exchange of goods and services across all borders. Things formerly forbidden under communism were now possible and accessible, including the people. With that openness came the chance to make anything happen in a way that was not possible before. By extension, because part of the debate was about economics, the economic system that was also closed when communism fell was also opened. Countries scrambled to invest overseas even as ethnic groups formerly under Communist domination similarly scrambled to form nations and declare their identities. The fall of communism heralded the opening of the world.

At the same time communism was falling, sophisticated technology became available to the average human being. Personal computers could be owned. Messages could be sent anywhere in the world using those computers. They became windows on the world. The ability to exchange not only conversation but also documents, books, video, and music, which just 10 years earlier was done slowly and with difficulty, could now be done at the speed of light anywhere in the world by anyone with access. The free flow of technology leads to the ability to make money in places that were formally inaccessible. Information could be gotten from places that could not be accessed before. Ideas could be exchanged with new groups of people.

Even with the openness of the political system, things still would have been kept local if there had been no sophisticated technology available. A case can be made that the information revolution took the form it did to meet the requirements of post-Communist politics and economics. A new openness called for things to replace the old. The technology acted as a facilitator for the exchange of new ideas, which in turn changed the political and economic system. Information is put out to other people in other places, which alters their perceptions of the world for good or ill in a way that is not possible without this information technology.

The technology that allows for this exchange of information facilitates the exchange of ideas on a global scale and allows people to connect with each other in ways not possible before. Having an idea of how the world should be, people can put it on a Web site and broadcast it globally. Others who agree with the position (and those who oppose it) will connect with each other. This has the effect of defining up front who are friends and who are enemies in a way that probably would not happen at a barbecue or political rally. Now, it can be done through technology: making contact, bringing together all the people who support an issue, and converting others. Each day is a step toward building a community that is both local and global and capable of fulfilling political goals.

One of the things most closely controlled in the in the cold war was the flow of ideas. There were many things that the Communists did not want their people to know about the West. It was considered dangerous to Communist control for people to know about Western freedoms. When communism fell, there was no one prohibiting the exchange of ideas. People began to find out that they were not alone in the world, that there are others who think like them. They can talk to each other every day, formulate plans, and move forward on a political agenda. The sum total of all of these things makes up a form of access that can be best called global connection and coordination or global access.

All the factors discussed here are equally necessary to make global access possible. If there was no open political system, the technology probably would not have a far-reaching effect. If there were no ideas flowing around the world, the open world system would not matter. If there were no technology, it would not matter what ideas people had or who they wanted to send them to, it would have to be a local phenomenon. All of these factors together have combined to make global access possible and make it the key that allows for the formulation of new communities, advancing new agendas, organizing funding, and training people to fight on behalf of those agendas. This is what this book is about.

The Importance of Context

By controlling context, issue organizations/groups decide the level of risk and reward, exposure, and expenditure for their planned action. They try to take as much or as little of each as they feel is necessary. We can look at the differences between insurgents and government forces to learn more about their interaction and the effects of context on that interaction. Context here is couched in the familiar questions: Who? What? When? Where? Why? How?

Who?

Who is fighting on each side? Where do they come from? What kind of people are they? Are they successful at war? Do they have idiosyncrasies that translate into strengths or weaknesses? What is their domestic political situation? What level of morale, training, and expertise does each side have? What are the relative advantages and disadvantages for each side? Knowing the answers to these questions can help in the decision regarding the degree to which unconventional forces will engage and what intensity the conflict may carry.

Insurgent forces	Government forces
Fighters can be indigenous, sent from outside, or outside volunteers. They are highly motivated or fanatical. They are trained broadly but not necessarily highly with some experts present.	Forces are dispatched at government need. They can be dedicated but not always motivated. They can be highly trained but for narrow duties. Few experts present, but more in support behind the scenes.

What?

What tools are in use on each side? If one side is relying on long-range weaponry, it may be best to engage them in places like cities or jungles, where only short ranges are available. If one side has equipment that relies on frequent replacement or resupply, it may be advantageous to fight in places where supply is a problem or to attack enemy supply. Is there a relative technological parity? If one side is technologically inferior, can it be rectified with available resources? If not, can fights take place in such a way that the technology is rendered useless? What resources are available to each side? A side with plentiful resources will be difficult to defeat, and the best outcome may simply be to avoid losing until parity is achieved or the costs of fighting outweigh the costs of leaving. Does any side have a numerical advantage? Numbers still count, and numerical advantage in forces means greater area and scope of operations for one side as well as more staying power, provided there is enough supply to sustain numerically large forces.

Insurgent forces	Government forces
Can be hi-tech, but not in a uniform way. Predominantly commercial technology, allows for rough parity. Fungible monetary resources (drugs, oil, etc.) decide degree. They can be augmented by other groups, but need not mass to fight.	Forces are uniformly equipped. Can be hi-tech depending on resources. They are not directly fundable. They count on revenue collection. Some direct funding of actions is a big advantage. Commercial technology is used but they mainly rely on developing own technology. They find comfort in massed forces. Western forces seek technological superiority.

When?

There are two facets to the timing of an attack. On the strategic level, it can be executed sooner or postponed until later. The choice is often predicated on an appraisal of relative weakness and opportunity. If the attackers are too weak to have a chance at success, they may defer. At the same time, if a weakness is found in the enemy, it may only be a weakness for a short time and so must be attacked at that point or an important opportunity is lost. On the operational level, an attack can also be made when both sides are alerted to impending fighting or when one side surprises another. Insurgent forces tend to make their attacks when they have surprise on their side because they are usually no match for government forces. Both insurgent forces and government forces operate in this way. However, as the section on organization illustrates, insurgent forces take better advantage of "when" than governments.

Where?

In choosing a location for action, one must bend to both geography and weather, which tend to affect all forces in the same way, all other things being equal. However, the choice of attacking or defending a location changes the context of action at that location. Here also, insurgents are organized better to either take advantage of location or stay clear of it, depending on perceived advantage, than slower government forces. This is because they need less in terms of supply and are quicker to assemble and move.

Why?

Part of deciding how hard to press an action and the intensity the action should have is knowing what the stakes are. Important stakes tend to make the execution of the attack more intense. Because stakes are a function of political goals, the ability to tailor actions directly to political goals builds intensity into the execution. Here also, issue organizations/groups have an advantage over governments. People in issue organizations/groups tend to be volunteers, and many of them are zealots for the cause to which they volunteer. Volunteer government forces also tend to a lesser degree to be more motivated to fight. Forces made up of conscripts or those pressed into service tend to be less motivated to fight.

How?

The actual operational/tactical fighting actions constitute the how. Here, the training of all forces comes into play. Highly trained forces are able to achieve tactical or operational objectives with greater efficiency. On the tactical/operational level of warfare, mistakes can be very costly. Well-trained forces will be less susceptible to mistakes and more successful in winning battles, all other things being equal. This is true for both insurgents and government forces.

Organization

Organization for war decides the potential ease, speed, and accuracy with which a given organizational unit takes action and takes advantage of the strategic context for action. An organization with many levels of authority built in, such as the hierarchy in all government forces, takes longer to assimilate incoming information, make decisions, order actions, and execute. Issue organizations/groups have fewer levels of authority involved in executing actions. Their power is less focused than government forces, but much more flexible. Looking at the level at which actions are performed, we see the following:

Insurgent forces	Government forces
When and why are given to actors. Those actors figure out who, what, where as well as how. Actions take fuller advantage of context and conform more fully to political goals. In this way, even operational loss in battle can be mitigated by the context set as part of the action plan.	Context is set above the level of action (operational/tactical) by higher authority. Actors only really get input for how they will fight after context is set. Results of action have weight only within preset context. If the context is poor, even winning the battle may not yield desired results.

Adaptability/Creativity

Adaptability and creativity go together. They are both a function of the knowledge and expertise available, allowing a given force to reconfigure itself to meet changing circumstances and find new and effective ways of doing things. In any war, things tend to be fluid, often seeming to take on a will of their own. Events can easily outrun intentions, and the so-called fog of war makes it difficult to predict the results of any action. Because this is true, the side that is best able to adapt to the fluidity will be ready at least to cope with changes without losing effectiveness. The side that is most creative has the best chance of creating situations where the enemy fails to adapt. Although both insurgents and governments are capable of adaptability and creativity, the following differences occur:

Insurgent forces	Government forces
Can have a variety of backgrounds and expertise. Although some duties may go unfilled in the short term, insurgent units may possess deeper expertise than governments in places. Insurgents can go out and obtain expertise they need more quickly and have fewer institutional barriers to change.	Even volunteer forces are given modes of service for its soldiers that are well defined and bounded. This guarantees that critical duties are identified and filled, but institutional problems make it difficult to identify and fill new needs quickly.

Why are insurgents successful at war in the modern era? Why do they seem to win their political goals even though they lose often in operational-level fighting? There are a number of historical episodes showing how insurgencies have been successful strategically even when they have been beaten operationally. It is worthwhile to make a short investigation of an event to demonstrate this.

Look at the Tet Offensive during the Vietnam War in 1968. The overall Communist goal of Tet was to sever the alliance between South Vietnam and America, possibly by taking over South Vietnam, but if not, by demonstrating to South Vietnam that their alliance with America had no ultimate hope of success (*Why?*).[3] The attacks were executed on a Vietnamese holiday during what was supposed to be a truce (*When?*). The attacks were mostly undertaken by seasoned Vietnamese Communist (Viet Cong) guerrillas augmented with North Vietnamese Army troops armed with small arms weaponry and operating all over South Vietnam (*Who?/What?*). Because all Viet Cong cells were activated they would fight all over South Vietnam, each in their own operating location. Within that framework, special attention was paid to attacking the symbols of the power of the old regime and of the United States, such as Hue City and the American Embassy (*Where?*).[4] In short, given the when and why for the Tet Offensive and some general guidance on where, Viet Cong cells filled in the context for their own individual attacks (*How?*).

The U.S. forces could only react to the attacks operationally and tactically. On that level, they defeated the Viet Cong at every turn, badly mauling the Viet Cong forces. The fact that Viet Cong resistance was shattered by the Tet Offensive was a secondary concern. The scope of the attacks, taken in the right context, had the desired effect, severely damaging America's alliance with South Vietnam and its support at home. Subsequently, President Johnson declined to run for a second term as president. He refused General Westmoreland's request to expand the war. American popular support evaporated. The Communists owned the context for the actions they took in the Tet Offensive, and so they were able to achieve some semblance of their goals even with operational defeat.

Thus, even operational defeat can yield favorable political results as long as the forces involved have the advantages of context, organization, adaptability, and creativity. In particular, it is important to orient to owning the strategic context of action. This is how insurgencies have been and are successful. This is how they can fight against powerful government forces and win. This idea is a departure from conventional warfare and its reliance on battlefield victory for advancing political goals, but its effectiveness cannot be denied as the next chapters show.

The Path Ahead

Issue organizations/groups are configured to be more directly efficient in pursuit of their goals than governments. They are able to prepare to act quicker and meet their needs quicker. Although they do not possess the power or wealth of the more powerful governments, they can still contend with them using war as the medium just as governments do. It is worthwhile to discuss briefly the capabilities governments use to go to war as a way of seeing how issue organizations/groups generate those same capabilities.

What has separated governments from other "agenda advancers" is the ability to focus a variety of capabilities on the agenda. Governments have authority over everyone and everything in their domain. Whether agreement or coercion flavors these capabilities, a government defines, represents, and advances the interests of the masses. A number of agendas can be advanced without going to war. Those agendas do not need or get the full support and participation of the largest part of the population. However, to go to war an agenda must be able to gain support from the masses. Thus, the first step in going to war is gathering and motivating a constituency. Then, capabilities can be mobilized to prepare and fight. This is how it has always been. What has changed is that governments no longer hold a monopoly on going to war. They are leadership, combat forces, combat support, and intelligence.

Governmental authority picks the direction for focusing the power and the agenda the masses will follow. That authority flows from a central government down through smaller bodies from states and provinces to national groups. The choice of agenda can be good or bad, possible or not, depending on how the agenda matches up with the leadership. For instance, the Roosevelt administration seems to have been capable of supporting an agenda aimed at overcoming the Depression. The population was mobilized behind an active president, willing to enact new programs such as unemployment compensation and Social Security, among others, to stabilize the economy. In contrast, Weimar Germany's leadership did not have as much success in that same Depression.

If authority is the hallmark of this model, then its first component can be identified as leadership. For governments, this involves a national leadership with a leader and advisers. The type of government is less important here as all governments have these features. Leadership in this case means the direction of assets to execute the agenda and the ability to mobilize those assets cohesively.

The national leadership defines the direction and boundaries under which all subordinate and subservient entities act. As long as actions are viewed either as supporting national agendas or beneath notice, they may continue. Any actions that do not support and could potentially injure the agenda bear watching and possibly counteraction. Thus (to speak in extremes), patriotic organizations and gardening clubs are acceptable, and revolution is not.

Setting the agenda seeks a result meant to enhance some aspect of the nation and its leadership. If successful, the result will give the leadership more tools with which to enhance its power. The fact that the leadership plans the agenda and that agenda is followed tends to reinforce its authority. Implicit in this authority is the capacity to mobilize capabilities within the governmental realm to advance the agenda. Finally, if the leadership is good at choosing agendas, the masses will mobilize their support, enhancing the chances of success, the prospective gain, and the authority of the leadership. Agenda setting is the most important power any government has, and as long as it is done productively, it is self-reinforcing.

Because war is an important tool of agenda advancement, nations field armed forces to fight to defend or advance the agenda on behalf of the nation. These forces are responsible for defending the nation. They also help keep internal order. In some regimes, they protect the government's interests abroad. Ideally, they do this over things that are not negotiable, but they can also do it as part of the bargaining position. Whatever the reason, armed forces are an important part of governmental power and allow for the survival and growth of both the agenda and the government. They are part of what makes governments able.

Being able only works when accompanied by knowledge. Knowing who is on our side is a function of interacting with the outside world. Certainly, one could define friends and enemies internally without interaction. Reality only comes through interaction, either openly through diplomacy or secretly through intelligence operations. National governments need to know the details of who their enemies are. This is why intelligence is such an important aspect of conducting war. Knowing capabilities will show potential competitors. Intentions reveal what they intend and whether their intentions are hostile. These capabilities speak to the ability of a government to lead people, pursue agendas, and alliances. Investigating capabilities reveals the strengths and weaknesses of the nation in digestible, quantifiable terms.

The armed forces (and the intelligence arms) of governments do not simply appear. Development of the armed forces can be broken into three parts: recruitment, training, and procurement. In an effective armed force, each of the three is not only necessary, but also dependent on the others for successful development. That is, the number of recruits affects how many weapons can be procured. The level of training affects how complex weapons can be. The cost and complexity of equipment will decide how many people to recruit up to a point.

Procurement includes all equipment, not just weapons. For sure, forces must have weaponry, but transportation and logistics support also must be available for soldiers and equipment alike. Training is going to be a function of the people a nation can recruit. A more educated population will respond to more sophisticated training (all other factors being equal). A less-educated population will still pick up some sophisticated training but will be hampered by a learning curve.

Raising an army is not just a matter of recruitment, training, and equipment. An army serving a nation is an arm of government. The soldiers are government employees on call every minute to defend the nation. They are moved in spite of their preferences where they are needed, setting down no roots, unlike other government employees. The government must provide for their care as the price for their obedience and handiness. They must be housed where they are sent. They must be paid so they can provide for their dependents.

They must be fed when on duty. They must have medical care. Governments provide for armies in this way to keep them together as a unit, ready to fight. Without this, desertion, dereliction of duty, and a breakdown in discipline would occur that would destroy the effectiveness of the force.

Much of this discussion is moot without funding. Since the days of ancient kings, all governments have struggled with the problem of paying for an army. All governments want the best armed forces on Earth but settle for the best armed forces money can buy. For the United States, this is good news because the American government has far more wealth than its competitors. The news is less good for other, poorer nations.

So, these are the forces governments use to go to war: leadership, combat forces, intelligence, and combat support. Each is now available to issue organizations/groups, breaking the monopoly national governments have had on them for centuries. They are accessible to anyone to pursue agendas apart from or in opposition to those of national governments. Issue organizations/groups can now field their own capabilities to wage war on behalf of their own political agendas.

The chapters that follow illustrate the features of this way of war. Chapter 2 will deal with mobilization and how communities are formed from issue organization actors and how executive functions arise to provide planning, direction, and message to the community. Chapter 3 explores how insurgents are engaging in warfare. This includes types of warfare, operations, and locations. Chapter 4 shows how agents engage in intelligence collection and analysis. Chapter 5 looks at combat support in terms of funding, training, and procurement. Having detailed how these governmental capabilities are now reproducible by issue organizations/groups and how they are used to advance agendas, a theory of global insurgency is developed in Chapter 6. Finally, in Chapter 7, we look at Al Qaeda as the first global insurgency.

Chapter 2

LEADERSHIP AND MOBILIZATION

One powerful global trend has arisen as a result of improvements in communications technology. Factions scattered around the world can unite to advance an issue on which they all agree. In ages past, every community may have had a faction that, given a chance, might have united over a given issue. Because communications until the 19th century were a function of traveling on foot or by horse, it was difficult to link up with like-minded people or even know that they existed. The radio, the telephone, and finally the Internet have allowed people supporting sympathetic issues to find each other and not only commiserate but also integrate into a network of mutual support. The openness of the political system in the world today means that the networks can branch out even further to include people supporting related issues in nations all over the world. This phenomenon has led to numerous combinations of organizations coming together to advance an issue and then in some cases breaking apart later. These issue convergences become joint ventures that allow for much more power and influence to be brought to bear on an issue than was possible before now.

The factions engaging in these joint ventures are heterogeneous. That is, they are different from each other and bring different capabilities to bear on an issue. They can cover each other's weaknesses or enhance each other's strengths. This creates a sort of synergy in which the components coming together generate more power than they would have singly. This phenomenon can expand depending on the issue. Issues bridge to other issues. This can bring in even more interested parties with their own capabilities. The scope of organizations and activities is also widened and can become worldwide overnight. Any faction connected to any related issue may join together with other factions to help each other. This means that defining a given network of cells or groups may become a function of tracking all of the issues that could connect together and then trying to see what organizations may enter the fray on behalf of each issue.

Various factions may bring various capabilities with them to advance the group agenda. Some may be good at public relations capabilities. Others may have access to needed resources. Still others may possess paramilitary forces. Together they can create an entity with global reach, a large resource base, and a variety of capabilities without being monolithic or easy to find. Such a network may well grow to possess capabilities that dwarf small nations, making it an important player on the world stage for a short or long time depending on the issue.

In 1994, an uprising started in Chiapas, Mexico. It arose from differences between rich and poor, lagging social reform, and land reform. In Chiapas, as has often been the case in Latin America, there is great disparity between rich and poor. The inequality in the distribution of land and wealth led to conflicts over who had power. In Chiapas, the situation had reached the point at which the residents of that land felt that they needed to act violently or lose all of their power.[1]

The Zapatista National Liberation Army (EZLN) declared the independence of Chiapas from Mexico. Obviously, this was a provocative move, and it got the expected response. Mexican government forces converged on Chiapas but with orders to tread carefully and seek intelligence on the situation before acting. The EZLN had other plans and attempted to force the issue with government troops in hopes of rallying other people in Mexico to their side.[2] Violence between them and government forces commenced, and the EZLN quickly found itself taking heavy casualties. They were losing, weakening, and quickly saw that violent action was not going to gain them any advantages.

At this juncture, nongovernmental organizations (NGOs) began to take interest in the plight of Chiapas. By 1993, there were nearly 200 NGOs in Mexico.[3] They had formed to advance a number of different agendas. Having formed, many came to the places where their issues were made real. First-hand observation of what was going on was the first step in reporting inequality and abuses to the rest of the world. As the world became less and less tolerant of these abuses, these NGOs gained more influence in the countries to which they journeyed. Many of these NGOs were seeking more autonomy and self-determination in places like Chiapas.

Soon, U.S. and Canadian NGOs joined in the insurrection, linking to the Chiapas independence issue by way of protesting against the

North American Free Trade Agreement (NAFTA) or other Latin American policy issues.[4] The fact that NGOs from outside Mexico had taken notice of the events in Chiapas was a victory of sorts for the EZLN. Subcommandante Marcos of the EZLN invited NGOs from around the world to come to Mexico and see what was happening.[5] He was unable to fight the Mexican government forces successfully but recognized that he might gain the support of world opinion if NGOs would rally to his side, even in a nonviolent way. When they did, the initiative clearly swung away from the Mexican government, if not fully to the EZLN. At the least, the Mexican government could not crush the rebellion with force in full view of the entire world. To do so would invite the backlash of a number of nations and potential investors.

These NGOs made demands that mirrored many EZLN demands.[6] This served to strengthen the position of the EZLN at the negotiating table by giving those demands support and legitimacy. At the same time, the incident at Chiapas served as a forum to illustrate the importance of the issues the NGOs were trying to advance. This transformed the Mexican government's position quickly from one of strength through authority and force to one of near parity at the negotiating table. Mexican cabinet ministers were stunned.[7] It was unprecedented for a network of unarmed groups to interfere in what amounted to civil war, especially successfully and nonviolently.

Many types of NGOs came to Mexico: human rights, ecumenical, indigenous rights, and infrastructure groups. In all, 34 groups came from outside Mexico to support the EZLN.[8] Chiapas served as a lens to focus all of the groups mentioned here into one group with one overall agenda comprised of several smaller agendas. The reasons for rebellion in Chiapas linked well with the issues these NGOs represented.

The shooting stopped once these NGOs came to Mexico, and stalemate set in. The Mexican government had not thought to confront all of the variety of groups that converged on Mexico. The EZLN gained not only publicity for their issue, but also a variety of capabilities and resources they did not have and could not have fielded on their own. The results were mixed. The EZLN survived, and the Mexican government was forced to negotiate with them. There has not been a solution, but there has been little bloodshed, which is certainly different from how things might have been.[9]

What happened in Chiapas implies certain things for modern conflict. The insurgents were quicker to organize and act than the Mexican government. Politics was able to trump the use of force when used correctly. Issues became a center of gravity or a battleground to control rather than actual land or governmental control. The insurgents were able to survive the violence because of these things. This may be true of future insurgencies also.

As another example, transnational criminal organizations (TCOs) are engaging in global cooperation to shore up weaknesses, lessen risks, and maximize gains in their enterprises. The fall of communism opened up a number of markets for the entrepreneurs of the world, including criminal entrepreneurs as well as legal ones. Communist nations had the apparatus to ensure internal security and were able to contend with or destroy many of the criminal organizations in those places. When Communist governments fell in the early 1990s, the internal security apparatus of those nations was either disassembled or fell apart because of lack of funds. This opened the whole of the world behind the Iron Curtain to new entrepreneurs of all types, criminals included.

These TCOs use partnerships with other criminal organizations to reduce profit loss, seizure of goods, and arrests. They also engage in partnerships to open doors to new markets quicker and easier than trying to do it alone.[10] This quickly makes each partner bigger than it could be on its own. Operations of much larger scale and scope are possible without having to generate the apparatus necessary for larger operations by a single partner. Instead, partners use each other's infrastructure and share supplies rather than fielding the costs of building another infrastructure or buying more inventory. One partner can gain easy access to markets it could not have had access to previously. Another partner can move much more inventory through its infrastructure than it has available without having to manufacture more. Each side gains more than it was possible to do alone. Each side shares the risks, which are dispersed among the partners.[11]

A clear example of this type of joint venture occurs in the Western Hemisphere drug trade. Mexican drug smugglers and Colombian drug suppliers cooperate to allow the Colombians access to American markets through existing Mexican networks rather than build their own. In return, Mexican smugglers get access to supplies of Colombian cocaine.[12] In this way, neither partner has to invest in anything new, and both partners gain more than they would have had alone.

There are other examples not limited to the Western Hemisphere. Mexican and Chinese TCOs partner in the smuggling of aliens into the United States. Mexican criminal organizations are well known for their involvement in smuggling illegal aliens across the U.S. border with some success. Chinese triads, rather than trying to build their own smuggling network, partnered with their Mexican counterparts to smuggle Chinese aliens to the United States as well. In a move mirroring that of the Mexican/Colombian partnership, Nigerian and

Colombian TCOs have partnered in a heroin/cocaine supply exchange.[13] This allows each side to establish a foothold in markets and to sell inventory they did not previously have. The Colombians can become involved in the heroin trade, and the Nigerians can gain access to Western markets. Colombian and Sicilian TCOs partner in heroin trafficking. This allows the Sicilians to gain access to markets lost in the West to the Chinese triads and gives the Colombians a chance to sell heroin in Europe. Sicilian and Russian TCOs have partnered with each other for money laundering.[14]

Linkages between TCOs and governments or terrorist groups have also been made. There is advantage in doing this to all concerned. The backing of a government supplies TCOs with safe havens from powerful nations and can supply them with resources, such as weapons that can be sold (more is said of this in chapter 5). At the same time, TCOs are able to perform services that are less than ethical for governments while allowing the government to appear clean. Connecting to terrorists gives TCOs power, intimidation, and resource backing for their ventures while providing the terrorists with a source of money and weaponry.[15]

These are transitory partnerships driven by need, risk aversion, or both. As such, they are not carved in stone. They exist while they are profitable and are dissolved when they fail to fill the need or avert the risk. Other joint ventures work along similar lines; however, other NGOs are more motivated to advance their agendas than criminal organizations are for any given partnership. Still, TCO cooperatives are difficult to oppose because they are dispersed and diversified. A criminal organization in one nation can be located, surrounded, and destroyed. A criminal organization spread out over several countries, partnered with other organizations, and involved in a number of activities will be much more difficult to stop.

In a different joint venture, protestors descended on Seattle, Washington, to protest a summit of the World Trade Organization (WTO) in 1999. This summit brought a number and variety of NGOs to Seattle to register their discontent with the widening emphasis on trade in the world, sometimes at the expense of addressing the way people must live. The importance of the summit in Seattle seemed to bring a number of groups to that city seeking to call attention to their causes. The protests were sometimes violent and succeeded in delaying the summit by snarling traffic.[16]

A diverse group of organizations took part in the protests. The AFL-CIO (American Federation of Labor and Congress of Industrial Organizations) sponsored a march of some 20,000 labor activists to protest the summit. That many people marching through a city cannot help but be disruptive even when peaceful. Once vandalism or violence starts and the police get involved, chaos can easily result. Thus, the protestors were able to delay the start of the summit and continually disrupt it. The international news media already present took notice, to the delight of the protestors.

The organization United for a Fair Economy attended, protesting that average people had no voice in this summit even though it would affect their lives. From San Francisco, the group Global Exchange came to advance human rights, living and wage standards, and the environment. The Teamsters came because they wanted organized labor represented at the summit. The Longshoremen Union was against unrestricted free trade and shut down West Coast cargo movement for a day in protest.[17] The Sierra Club came to protest how the WTO was handling environmental and food safety issues. The Earth Justice Legal Defense Fund came because it felt that the WTO emphasized trade over environmental and human health concerns.[18] This was an eclectic group of NGOs brought together by way of world trade policy and how it affects their issue interests. Some were violent, breaking windows and so forth. Most, but not all, attempted to disrupt the conference in some way to advance their issues to consideration.

The issue component linkage in these three cases is important here. To define the linkages in each case, an analyst can note the issue, who links to it, why, and for how long. In this way a defined entity can take shape along with its purpose and possible capabilities. What is also important is to see the event that causes the NGOs to form the joint venture. That event is the key from which everything else can be tracked and subsequent strategy can be generated. In Chiapas NGOs that supported human rights, democracy, and land reform as broad issues found a place to take a stand in support of the EZLN. Chiapas is an example of a specific issue acting as a lens to focus multiple NGOs and call world attention to a number of interconnected agendas for long or short durations.

TCOs all have the same broad issues: acquisition and risk reduction. This leads to their transitory partnerships. In this case, opportunity to operate under the above conditions was the lens focusing their efforts. Yet, as stated, because there is no issue that motivates the TCO beyond gain, the partnerships are transitory. They are together as long as both are willing to do their part or one side no longer needs the other.

The WTO protests brought together a patchwork quilt of environmental, labor, and human rights groups. The broad issue of how people will live and work as a result of the WTO summit brought diverse elements together to advance multiple interconnected agendas. The summit acted as the lens focusing the NGOs, but they melted away after the summit.

There are both advantages and disadvantages readily apparent in these joint ventures that will be seen over and over. The advantages come from the realms of survivability and adaptability. For instance, NGO networks cannot be easily defeated by decapitation of leadership or simple attrition. The vacuum created by either of these two strategies will be quickly filled by others. These networks evaporate and reconfigure easily to new shapes, tailoring to the needs of the moment. They also allow backers of the network to maintain anonymity because tracking components of a network can be a complicated process with built-in deniability. The disadvantages spring from the realm of loyalty and cohesion. Factions may push and pull against each other for preeminence. There may be loyalty issues of the type associated with coalition governments. When a faction within the network is satisfied, they may leave. Backers can be discomfited by the actions of the network and that also can cause them to leave.

Before continuing this discussion, a disclaimer is probably in order. Peaceful NGO protests, the Chiapas insurgency, TCOs, and Al Qaeda are all under discussion in the same breath as examples of changes in leadership, organization, and mobilization on the grassroots level. It is not intended to lump them all together as the same type of organization. But, all of these examples serve a purpose by illustrating the behavior of nonstate organizations. All of these organizations are examples showing alternate forms of organization and agenda setting to the traditional governmental examples. They all have some element of global scope and are not simply contained within a single nation. This shows their eclecticism and worldwide reach. They all have agendas and motivations that differ from those of any single national government.

Yet, they are different. The WTO protestors are not the same as the Chiapas insurgents. Moveon.org (an organization that brings other organizations together to form grassroots movements) is not the same as Al Qaeda. It is unlikely that Al Qaeda leadership or even middle management will sit down and explain to the world at large how they organize and mobilize. That is fine. This subject is broader than Al Qaeda. There are wider possibilities than just Al Qaeda, and it is best to show those possibilities rather than just limit the investigation to one organization.

We can acknowledge that Moveon.org facilitates the gathering of diverse organizations to engage in protests and political activism regarding various issues. At the same time, a case can be made that Al Qaeda is the dark side of global political activism. They facilitate the gathering of organizations to engage in insurgency. We have seen that some connection has arisen between Al Qaeda and Al Zarqawi-led insurgents in Iraq.[19] In Indonesia, a group with Al Qaeda ties is doing relief work for victims of the tsunami.[20] Al Qaeda is in many other places facilitating the gathering of more organizations to its cause. So, although it is not being alleged that Moveon.org or peaceful NGOs are the same as Al Qaeda, the techniques they use to organize diverse peoples for political action are effective. It is not a great leap to suggest that future insurgencies will exhibit the same tendencies as any of the organizations discussed here.

There are immense implications here for the U.S. "war on terrorism" or any future war like it. Anyone can see in reading about NGO joint ventures that fighting a war against such an entity changes the nature of the war from anything the modern era has known. This is no longer war against a traditionally definable enemy. There are many partners fighting against the United States. It is certain that not all of them are known and equally certain that the motives of all of these partners are not clearly understood. Until these things are known, it is unclear how successful the United States will be in prosecuting global insurgencies.

The United States is currently attacking the Taliban and Al Qaeda (a "terrorist organization") in Afghanistan. It is probable that there are many more partners to those two groups scattered around the world. Indeed, that network may really be comprised of all of the factions in the world that oppose the way the United States leads world initiatives. Tracking down the lens focusing these groups will also be difficult. Basing American forces in Saudi Arabia may be the lens that focused insurgents on the September 11th attacks, but it could also be something important to anti-United States, anti-Zionist, anti-globalist, anti-free market, or anti-equal rights groups. Indeed, any of those potential lenses may draw some or all of the potential non-state organizations listed here to support attacking the United States. Add in the power seekers rejecting old regimes, directing wrath against the United States and nearly every Moslem government, and the picture gets less and less clear. Many factions worldwide are probably supplying intelligence, resources, and agents to Al Qaeda. The network is too big and too dispersed to be destroyed by monolithic, hierarchical governments using conventional means. If one accepts this logic, another way of prosecuting this conflict, one that takes counsel of NGOs and global insurgency, becomes necessary.

The examples cited here are less about fighting and more about managing conflict in which actual fighting can be a component. The type of conflict management non-state organizations in these examples use is different from the way governments operate. The differences can be found in organization, motivation, leadership, and mobilization, among other things. It is important to understand how and why these differences can result in effectiveness and understand how and why these organizations are able to engage in conflict. There are some common characteristics to keep in mind for global insurgencies: They are driven by issues; they seek partnership; they have a transitory nature; they are flexible, survivable, and quick. These characteristics separate the organizations discussed here from governments. It is the first of these, the issue-driven characteristic, that may be the most important to analyze because it is the issue that holds various cells or groups together.

Issues and Their Characteristics

Issues can be broadly classified into those supported and those not supported by governments. As stated in Chapter 1, governments support issues that enhance their power and status. These issues include nationalism, balance of power, and the like. Not all issues can be supported by governments. Limited resources mean choices are made. Governments choose issues that cover the whole nation. Issues that do not affect the majority get little or no support.

Unaddressed issues tend to become grassroots popular movements. Some movements will be peaceful, aimed at civil rights; others can be a basis for civil war. This can happen in any nation. Some grassroots issues occur in a number of nations and become global. Even if issue supporters are a minority in one nation, the issue can transcend that nation to other nations. If enough nations have people who are minorities who support the issue, the minorities themselves can band together and have power. Broad international appeal brings the globalization of local issues. This means these issues can change governments and the world. These issues appear on the news and take forms like employment, environment, and religion. An indicator of which issues are important but not on government agendas comes from the list of NGOs one can find on the United Nations Web site. The site lists NGOs oriented to various issues. Although there are many issues that attract NGOs, the ones that attract more are of most interest. Here are some important issues and the number of NGOs oriented to those issues[21]:

Human rights	163 organizations
Development	155 organizations
Peace and security	112 organizations
Environment	68 organizations
Religion	63 organizations
Disarmament	58 organizations

All of these issues have to do with the quality of people's lives in some way. They also seem to be issues that governments either take no stand on or take a stand that is opposed by people outside government.

For an issue to be important, it must be important enough for a segment of the population to mobilize and act. Mobilization in isolation is not global. For mobilization to be global, the people mobilizing in each country must be connected. The connection is important. It allows information exchange. It can be used for education, training, and coordination of actions. This connection is the key to globalizing an issue. Without it, proponents of the issue become isolated and defeated piecemeal. With the connection, those same pockets have resiliency. This is because the idea always survives somewhere as long as there are proponents of it somewhere in the world with a connection to each other. Collective action worldwide also enhances the issue. "Thinking globally and acting locally" takes on new meaning in this vein. Different factions in different places support a broad agenda for their own reasons. The collective weight of these factions gives the issue salience. This makes the factions powerful.

Different factions in different places may support a broad agenda for their own reasons. For instance, organized labor and environmental groups banded together and formed the Citizens Trade Commission (CTC) to oppose NAFTA in 1993. The CTC had as members the Teamsters, United Auto Workers, Friends of the Earth, National Family Farm Coalition, and the Methodist Board of Church and Society, among many other organizations.[22] For many other issues, these organizations might not join, but for NAFTA they did, diversifying the outlook, goals, and effort.

Diversified membership means each faction will act in its own way. The flavor of that action will be a function of the politics surrounding the issue and the political system in which each faction operates. Every faction must work within a national or international political system. The character of that system brings groups to advance agendas either within or outside that system. The politics of the issue may place restrictions on action. Most notably, it may decide whether the action will be violent or nonviolent. Working within or outside the system is tricky. Protests, petitions, and letters are considered working inside a democratic system. However, in any totalitarian régime, those same things are considered working outside the system, and they can come with a larger punishment attached. In a democracy, violence against people or property is considered working outside the system. The importance of the issue and the possibility of gain decide the nature of the action, the amount of sacrifice, and the amount of exposure people will have when advancing that issue. Whichever path is chosen, support will be gathered, and membership will be achieved to a lesser or greater degree.

As the issue gathers support, machinery can be built to act on an agenda. This machinery will take the form of organizations, funding, and conferences. Which choice among types of actions (violence or nonviolence) comes down to the confidence actors have in the system. The actors must deal with the enforcers of the system and the response they will get in choosing violent or nonviolent action. For instance, Indian nationalists used nonviolence to gain independence from Britain. It is not clear that this strategy would have worked if India had to gain independence from the Nazis. They may have needed violence to secure their freedom.

Violence can be used at any time without provocation, and it seems to be used by reasonable people as well as the unreasonable. When it is perceived that their agenda must be fulfilled and they see that the agenda cannot be fulfilled under the system as it stands, violence can become an option, although it is not always so. At that point, a decision must be made by some or all factions in the following way. Either the system must be radically changed, or the system must be destroyed and rebuilt. In the event of either of those two conclusions, violence can often be the means to that end. Yet, the violence should not be chosen whimsically. It is largely a function of the idea that people cannot live as they have any longer. There are many examples of this, including the American Revolution, the French Revolution, the English and American Civil Wars, and the Boxer Rebellion in China.

In the past, important issues in a single nation sometimes brought violent responses from a unified nongovernmental group. Now, issues that transcend all nations are attracting people's attention and action. When these issues transcend nations, they become issues of global importance, such as when American environmentalists joined with Chilean activists to oppose the building of a lumber mill in Chile.[23]

As a result, the factors affecting these issues become global by default because more than one organization in more than one place is involved. Indeed, much of what is occurring in terms of protest and violence around the world has something to do with globalism on some level. The protests and the violence become global as a result. For example, the Seattle protests against the WTO, the antiwar protests against the Iraq war, and Al Qaeda are all examples of global movements against some aspect of action being taken by a nation or nations.

Organization

Any movement must have organization. The nature and the effectiveness of that movement depend on these things: who is to be directed, how, and to what end. There are two ways readily apparent that someone could organize for these global efforts. One way is centralized, and the other way is through a decentralized network or committee. Much has been written about network forms of organization, particularly (lately) the idea that they are superior to previous forms of organization. There is much to recommend a network as a way of organization and direction, but hierarchies also have advantages. Also, no one looking at hierarchies versus networks should be doctrinaire about which is better. It is possible even to use elements of both together and to be effective.

Governments and armed forces use hierarchy. This form of organization establishes clear responsibility and who has the power to make decisions. Insurgencies and global movements use committee forms of organization. Committees are known by characteristics such as consensus, membership, speed, and flexibility. Committees still use some semblance of authority to guide action. At the WTO protests in Seattle, it was noted that hierarchy was used for coordination, although not direction of participant's action. Instead, one commentator stated: "Our model of leadership was decentralized and leadership was invested in the group as a whole. People were empowered to make their own decisions and the centralized structures were for coordination, not control."[24] Each group apparently judged its own situation and acted according to agreed-upon responses. Committee direction allowed for all factions to have a voice and support decisions energetically.

With a hierarchy, establishing authority and responsibility within and across armed forces or governments is very complex but necessary. This speaks to the difference between hierarchy and the committee. Indeed, it can be likened to the difference between a pack of dogs and a team of dogs. A pack of dogs roams and hunts. This is good for subsistence and security by spreading the coverage and spreading the risk of failure to find food or survive attack. A team of dogs, on the other hand, can take a person and supplies across Alaska in a way that a pack cannot. Each has merits. Each is effective in the right context. Hierarchy is good for focus, and a committee is good for flexibility.

Committees attract the willing. Issues attract motivated groups who want to contribute. Such groups require a comfort zone so that their views will be heard, their agendas will be met, and their contributions (in whatever form) are accepted. The inclusion a committee-based authority provides is a key to insurgency warfare, such as when the Zapatista movement became larger and stronger by including other organizations in their struggle and vice versa.[25] Power comes from popular support. The popular support is generated by related agendas across all groups worldwide, all helping all to achieve those agendas. Hierarchy is still used, but it does not dictate action; it coordinates and guide action. This is done based on previously agreed-upon parameters for all groups participating in an event.

In organization, there is always some form of hierarchical authority. This also hints at the need for some level of conformity. Even within diverse groups, coordination requires some degree of consensus regarding what the group is going to do. The consensus gives a sort of authority of the whole over the parts, such as when in the WTO protests in Seattle protestors were asked to agree to nonviolence guidelines.[26] However, there is no discipline in a committee as in a hierarchy. Those not willing or able to conform may leave.

Reflecting on previous examples, committee-based organization forms around an issue and the problem it represents. The committee draws strength from the number of people joining. The object at the beginning is simply to connect with other people or organizations (local actors on an issue or issues) or groups (combinations of cells) that are in agreement with each other on the same issue. These cells/groups form an inner circle that begins to advance an agenda. Any issue can be broadened to connect with other issues that also have organized support.

In connecting to these other issues, other cells/groups become involved as common cause brings together diverse people with the same basic agenda. We can call this an *issue constellation* because groups appear connected from one point of view but do not appear connected from other points of view. These groups may come together for a given event and part company after the event when being together no longer serves the agenda of individual groups. Diverse groups can come, contribute, withdraw, and leave. Their contribution can be as low-key as supplying names to a petition or as important as supplying capability needed for the success of the operation.

Issue constellations gather many contributions from many groups with diverse capabilities in a variety of locations to allow wider coverage of an issue, and they allow participating group members to have access to much more capability than any one cell/group possesses. This means that the strong and the weak can contribute what they are able and draw strength from each other. The examples at the beginning of this chapter ably illustrate this concept. The protests in Seattle against the WTO, the Zapatista movement in southern Mexico, and even transnational criminal organizations are involved in this sort of organization. Furthermore, the examples show that contributions include a variety of actions, from public relations to communications to expertise.

The goals of the constellation motivate the service. Issue organizations/groups gather to collaborate for their own reasons. Jobs With Justice, for instance, uses pledge cards to commit to supporting other organizations' events. This has the effect of building mutual support among related organizations.[27] On the other hand, the EZLN in Chiapas was struggling for their homes and way of life and would have done so alone, if unsuccessfully. These two examples illustrate two basic reasons for collaboration: to gain resolution to an issue or an answer to a particular problem or to participate just to gain credibility on an issue. On the other hand, other groups collaborate in the name of reward. They are seeking tangible benefits from the action that will directly enhance their power and status.

The distinction between resolution motivation and reward motivation goes a long way in deciding who will stay with the issue for the long term and who will not. Organizations seeking a resolution may leave when they have it. The distinction also indicates which methods will be used for one action or another.

Who will stay or go is one of the more interesting aspects of the constellation. As the Zapatista and TCO examples illustrate, not all cells/groups who participate stay through to the conclusion of an event. A government would not tolerate that from its bureaucracy. Hierarchies need the predictability that comes from formal capabilities under their command. Because the issue constellations are not governments, they do not require such commitments. Participating organizations convene and decide on desired outcomes. They then decide which actions they will take to achieve those outcomes. Part of the decision process is deciding whether peaceful or violent means will be used.

When these decisions are made, they will have the effect of both attracting and repelling participants. Care must be taken not to alienate large segments of participants as these decisions are made. As for whatever the event is going to be, the organizations/groups that decide to participate will gather and begin building a relationship with each other, that is, a mutual benefit through the use of mutually reinforcing capabilities. Each component contributes what it can to gain that benefit.

Some cells/groups leave when their goal is achieved and no additional benefit can be achieved for them by staying. New issues can arise in the middle of events, or changes can take place that will reveal new opposition. This may attract or repel new organizations/groups as the event unfolds. It is possible that some may even come to safeguard their agenda from being hijacked by other members of the constellation.

This hints at the idea that organizations/groups may work together with each other, but they do not necessarily agree with each other on all things. Reward-seeking organizations/groups seek tangible power, money, and influence. Because of that, they are more likely to be around all the time rather than occasionally. Indeed, it is unlikely that they would leave a particular issue easily, if at all. These will be the cells/groups most likely to fight and sacrifice in the name of the issue.

There seems to be no animosity about component organizations/groups leaving early. It may be that reward-seeking organizations/groups do not necessarily want to share all of the reward or may simply be that there is no sense in keeping people around beyond their ability to contribute adequately.

The eclectic nature of organizations/groups is not simply about their goals. Many organizations/groups come in different sizes and have different motivations. Small ones will think locally and act globally. When they participate in these constellations, it will be to connect and coordinate with others to augment their own strengths. Large organizations can be national or global entirely by themselves, with affiliates in many places around a country or the world. Again, there is no formality.

Leadership

Simply having loose associations or, worse still, a mob, is not effective. Organization has been a part of history for so long because it is so effective, particularly in times of chaos like war. Whatever model of organization is used, someone or some entity must be the moti-vator for action, or to put it more plainly, the organization needs leadership. This leadership must make sure capabilities come together effectively to take the right action for the situation. They craft the messages that explain positions, justify actions, inform actors, and recruit supporters. Leadership can be controlling, as in a hierarchy, or coordinating, as in a committee. Whichever form it takes, it is im-portant as a glue to hold components together and as a motivator of collective action.

To attract participants and guide action, a leadership must craft a message. The message is important for people advancing an issue. It does a number of things. It guides participants. It explains positions on the issue. This may attract more people to come and support the issue. It gives meaning to actions and events. It defines end goals. The message also has an effect on the opponents of an issue. It defines opponents for the undecided. It defines the meaning of their actions. Defining the opponent can be very effective in recruiting, particularly if potential recruits want to believe the worst about the opposition, a difficulty American forces face in Iraq.

The message can call for active or passive support. Active support can take the form of assembly or call to use violence. On the other side of the spectrum, passive support could be signing a petition or simply going to a Web site and registering hits there. The message can be broad or specific, depending on the support sought. A distinction should also be made between general versus event messages. The general message will be about overall philosophy and is designed as a constant beacon for generating support. The event message, on the other hand, relates actions taken to reinforce the issue philosophy. This way, all know the who, what, where, when, why, and how of the action as it relates to the overall agenda. It tells whether the event will be violent. It tells whether the event will be focused on something specific. In many ways, this part of the message decides participation, association, and recruitment for the issue.

Returning to the leadership discussion, the following can be said: Committees are used to obtain input from contributors and generate decisions. Aspects of hierarchy are used to guide and coordinate the actions of the many. The message makes sure that the actions of the committee and the actions of opponents are all placed in the con-text of the issue and the philosophy surrounding it. In this way, talk is important—so is action.

Taking action requires knowing participants on an issue and what talent they have to contribute. This is different from the formality of a hierarchy, in which the capabilities are cataloged by function. These committees or issue constellations can be ad hoc. Some discovery is necessary. Because membership is not formalized, members and capabilities may come and go. A discovery process is needed to find out who is willing to do what. It also unearths the limits participants may set on their participation. Assignments are made based on who can meet the need of the issue set by the leadership. A socialization process takes place by which groups conform to the need of the issue to get rewards. Socialization spreads to coordinating action and support. As groups interact and discover each other's strengths, an organization evolves; roles are then created and filled. Cadres may guide the course of events, but participants drive the action. The question then becomes how do the political issue, and attending planning, coincide to yield action.

Activation

Once the issue convenes interested parties, the message is crafted, and roles are decided, information must then be transferred to activate participants. This activation does not happen from the top down. That would take too long, and the message would be diluted. Instead, participants need to be armed with the same information and be on the same page at the same time. Activation must be done all at once for all participants. This preserves the speed and flexibility needed by these issue constellations to take action. The message and the attending plan must be delivered to interested parties. In this way, the message gives guidelines for conduct and expected results. Participants need this information to fill goals of both the individual and collective agendas related to the issue. If they must know this to act and must all activate at once, they must be given all the information at the same time.

Activation all at once has never been easier than it is now because of information technology. Information can be transmitted by Web page, Web log (blog), Listserve, e-mail, or text messaging, among many other mediums. Obviously, not all are used equally. Web pages work best to activate things surrounding an event. An example of this would be a group of protestors called the Billionaires whose Web site allowed participants to download information to have their own Billionaire-style protests local to their area.[28]

People may not set up computers in protests or violent activities, and this makes them less useful in action. Cell phones and text messagers seem to be better during an event. Cell phones and text messaging aid speed and adaptability needed by an issue constellation to do what it has set out to do. An example of this would be when Philippine president Jose Estrada was ousted from power when a million people converged on Manila to protest against his administration. The protestors were coordinated by text messagers.[29]

It is possible for supporters to use Web-based communications while people on scene would use cell phones and text messaging for communications. This hints at command-and-control possibilities. Transmitting activation using modern communications is what allows diverse and dispersed groups to coordinate quickly.

Coordinating activities is what allows for geographically separate groups to take global action. The action is more properly broken into preparation, support, and event execution. Preparation always goes on, and it may also be known as day-to-day operations. Support and execution aim at action and are used to support or advance an agenda, going from each according to their talent to the needs of the issue (to paraphrase Karl Marx). Again, this coordination is not hierarchy: It may be more along the lines of a "hub and nodes" as Andrew Boyd wrote of the Billionaire protests: "The hub played an essential role shaping and steering the campaign. The hub designed the core ideas and launched the call to action."[30] This further implies that authority is used for coordination rather than direction. As an example, the people involved in taking action are involved in putting up tents that can be broken down and moved easily rather than putting up buildings, which cannot.

Because committee-based coordination is not mired in formality, it can be reconfigured and adapted. It can be made to fit the need of the issue. It also is able to adapt as and if the need changes. Why is that? Flexible use of talent not only according to need but also according to contribution is part of the reason. This is not an easy thing to do because there is a lack of permanence. But, because the action is directed at advancing an issue (rather than building a nation), it does not need to be permanent. Because the participants are willing, with similar goals to achieve, synchronization is easier. It is worthwhile to explore the nature of this synchronization to know what is and is not capable of advancement.

The synchronization of effort is necessary to any type of agenda advancement, but the character of synchronization changes with each organizational type. The transmission of information and instructions follows a different process for different organizations. In hierarchy, transmission originates at the top and filters down to the bottom. It becomes diluted and interpreted on the way as each leadership level puts its spin on the information. The lowest level of leadership has no big picture, only the information needed to do the job. The advantage of this is that it ensures that everyone knows their job and their role. The disadvantage of this is that it is slow and less responsive to change.

In a decentralized model, such as the committee model discussed here, activation informs actors on the lowest level of action. It skips the other levels, which in some cases do not exist, and avoids the dilution and interpretation of information that happens in a hierarchy. This also leads each cell or group to interpret things in its own way. In a hierarchy, this could cause problems, but in issue constellations, it is less of a concern. As long as the actions taken by any given organization or group fit the overall guidance and issue, some success is achievable. The advantage of this is that there is much less time lag to activate members of the constellation, who are better able to adapt and reconfigure themselves to events on the fly. The disadvantage of this is that it can be chaotic to do this without clearly defined roles and responsibilities. That means there must be some agreement among cells, groups, or recognized cadres.

To avoid this chaos, indoctrination and agreement on rules of engagement is a key for effective activation. This indicates that some aspects of hierarchy seep in to issue constellations for certain purposes. This arrangement allows more choices to be made with flexibility. It also allows organizations/groups to act with one purpose on the same basic thing. This is especially advantageous now when situations are fluid and require flexibility. It also works well in forms of conflict for which goals are more political than military.

Part of what this discussion is about is command and control, the means by which information is turned into action. How is the information actually transmitted? That is, by what physical means can it be done? Messages can be transmitted by open air or by technological tools. Transmission by open air uses coded phrases aired on open radio or television as a signal to act. For example, the French resistance was activated over BBC radio to support the D Day invasions. It has often been said that tapes released by Osama bin Laden have activation messages embedded in them. Of course, Web sites, e-mail, cell phones, and text messaging can also be used as discussed in the Activation section. This form of activation has the effect of reaching people in large numbers simultaneously. It hints at the ability to synchronize groups or organizations globally. Contrast activation in this way versus word of mouth.

No global effort would be possible without the ability to contact many people simultaneously; without it, there would not even be any knowledge that the issue exists globally. Modern communications grants access to all and allows contact among people worldwide on an individual level. This allows the type of mobilization discussed here to take place. This is not just about information technology. The character of the politics and the way to organize to meet the politics of an issue are about people and interaction at least as much as about information technology.

Because these constellations are not trying to be a government, they use existing infrastructures and means rather than building their own. They canuse spokespeople as much as leaders. They use ideological guidance rather than direction and orders. They adapt to the needs of the moment rather than force the moment to conform to their ways of doing things. Bear in mind that they seek simply to be effective. Because of this, they do not need the same machinery, practices, or proficiencies to achieve their goals.

Conclusion

How effective can issue constellations be? To answer this question, one must judge the goals of issue constellations and the degree to which they are achievable. The goals are inclusion, expansion, and issue dominance. Inclusion means the widest participation among issue supporters. This participation brings more resources to bear on the problem. Expansion is about influence spreading to new places. The more access and visibility one can obtain by expanding, the better possibility that the participants can feed the inclusion. Issue dominance is about making one's own version of the issue accepted and defended to more supporters in more places. Dominating a global issue gives the dominators global power, and if everybody agrees with one interpretation of the issue, the people who own the interpretation win. No one will be able to address or solve the issue in question without the influence of the dominators being felt. It may be a cause for war depending on how the dominators view things.

Because these goals are less specific than taking land or overthrowing governments, there are some changes of perception to be observed. There is less need for focus, hierarchy, or standing armies. This makes issue constellations more effective in some ways. Governments, on the other hand, have much more specific goals. They orient specifically to other nations to address balance of power and other such things. The attending specifics call for focus and direction in a way the issue constellations do not. They need standing military forces that also call for well-defined end states and procedures. Neither governments nor their armed forces are designed to do well with generalities.

Witness how much better the United States has handled interstate war than insurgency. This implies that things governments do in a conventional war tend to enhance the effectiveness of issue constellations fighting insurgencies. Focus on one issue leaves opportunity for others to exist away from the focus. Formality can also be rigidity. Hierarchy moves slowly to decide and act. It is difficult for anyone with these characteristics to be successful against an opponent who is fast, flexible, and everywhere.

This does not mean that governments and armies are destined for defeat. They can still compete. Their resources are plentiful. They can make available more resources, and their ability to focus is a powerful tool. However, to be effective in this type of war, they must use their focus more in the context of the issue. They must craft their own message and make sure that it relates to the issue.

It is important to understand that these issue constellations are not rivals to governments. Issue constellations do not try to take state power, or at least they have not so far. These are grassroots movements, intended to convince people to join them globally to support the issue (as with the WTO protests), not to overthrow governments. Issue constellations do not produce their own things. They use what governments produce: weapons, money, and infrastructure. People in these cells/groups are citizens of nations, and they live off the welfare of the governments of those nations. Issue constellations are rivals to governments for control of an issue, and they will try to use that control to change the course of government action. They draw strength from issues that transcend governments, and they rise and fall with the salience of these issues. The fact that these issues transcend governments allows the issues to be global in the first place. They are also what allow the violence attending those issues to be called war. What, in the past, would have been isolated insurgencies have now (because of politics and technology) allowed people to connect both physically and philosophically to become global insurgencies.

This type of global warfare must be insurgency because the issue constellations can never achieve the focus of governments. They cannot achieve physical focus because of the dispersal of people across large distances, and they cannot achieve political focus because of the diversity of groups involved in the issues that they are all serving, some of which are related but not identical. Issue constellations are physically weaker than governments for this reason. Because of that, they must deal with warfare in terms of insurgency rather than in terms of building their own standing army and taking over governments.

Indeed, fulfilling an issue agenda is easier than overthrowing a government. How much more so for trying to overthrow many governments? Fulfilling an issue facilitates inclusion, expansion, and issue dominance. This makes for a model of warfare that is more political, and the action must conform to the issue, the agenda, and the message. The question of who is with us is as important as who is against us. That said, this is not a bloodless model of conflict. Violence satisfies political agendas, and many issues in the future will have violence attached to them.

Chapter 3

GLOBAL INSURGENCY WARFARE

Chapter 2 discussed how diverse, dispersed non-state organizations (NGOs) came together to support issues. Part of their power to survive and fight lay in their dispersal. But, dispersal is not usually how people fight. Indeed, dispersal has not usually been considered an advantage. The history of warfare has been about the clash of armies on a battlefield for control of land or people. Dispersal in that type of war allows an army to be defeated piecemeal. Tradition says that to fight wars one must mass forces. Only by massing combat power can one win a decisive battle or even survive the attempt. Unifying command in a hierarchical structure from leader to soldier goes hand in hand with massing forces. In this way, large numbers of land or sea forces can be controlled and articulated together. Any admiral or general on Earth will verify that this has been the common practice.

Massing forces requires time and large resource expenditure. In the Gulf War, it took many months to transport troops and equipment to the Middle East. Once there, it took more time to train and prepare for war in the desert. Against another army that also needs time to mass and prepare, it is feasible to go to war in this way. In an insurgency in which timely action is a requirement for victory slow pace delivers no advantage. Likewise, unified command allows little flexibility to adapt to local situations in a timely manner. In a command structure in which information flows up through levels of authority to a single decision maker and orders flow down the same structure from a single decision maker to many soldiers in the field, there is little room for adaptability or quick action.

If the traditional way of war is too slow and too inefficient compared to insurgency, why use it? The traditional way of war allows for mobilization and focusing of national power in a way that facilitates the winning of contests for land and national power. In other words, if the objective of the war is to defeat another army and occupy land, this is the way to do it. Certainly, this is the way many wars have been fought across recorded time, but not all wars have been fought this way. Some wars, particularly civil wars, have been occasionally fought using unconventional means. Also, some wars have been fought for limited objectives for which the full mobilization of national power has not been necessary or desirable on any side.

Thus far, nonstate actors have not sought national power. It has been unnecessary and in some ways detrimental for them to do this. Witness what is going on in the Palestinian territories right now. When the Palestine Liberation Organization (PLO) was an insurgent organization, it was difficult to find and attack. The only way the Israelis could bring the PLO to a decisive battle was to invade nations where it was hiding, like Lebanon. Now, the PLO has formed a government and has a capital. Each time an attack is made on Israel traceable to Palestinian extremists, the Palestinian government has been held responsible by Israel and attacked. As a government, there is nowhere for them to hide from this. As an insurgency, there were always options for avoiding punishment.

Dispersal and Eclecticism

Because their goals lay outside gaining national power, organizations practicing insurgency can disperse using infiltration and surprise attack to fight for their objectives. This dispersal runs counter to accepted practice of conventional warfare and yet is effective. The reason insurgency works has to do with the idea of the diverse portfolio. Just as investors will spread their money into different stocks to lessen the risk of loss and maximize chances for success, insurgents will do the same thing. It is a strategy that allows for losses with mitigation. Insurgents have a more precarious position than nations. They have no stronghold, no safe place in which to reside and defend if attacked. If they concentrated anywhere, they could be located and destroyed. Dispersing their assets allows insurgents to survive overall even if some are destroyed in a given area.

Let us return to the stock-trading example. Concentration of assets in one stock can be dangerous unless you buy exceptionally strong ones. Concentrating all assets in a weak stock can be catastrophic, resulting in the loss of all assets in a short time. Buying strong stocks means there is less (but not no) chance of taking such a loss. Events are always in motion, and the strongest single stock can slowly devalue until it is no longer worth what it was when it was bought. Diversifying a portfolio spreads the risk so that if some of the assets perform badly, others may perform well and pick up the slack. Conversely, if all of the assets perform well, more money is made than if just one stock was bought and performed well. This strategy allows weathering a catastrophe in oil futures by also investing in, say, orange juice and computer chips.

Likewise, in war concentration works for powerful forces but not for lesser ones. For a weaker force, concentration can be a death sentence in the face of a superior force. Even for a strong force, sometimes concentration can be a risky proposition. If the war waged is based entirely on the existence of the army or navy, concentration is a risk. The risk is that if that force is defeated and destroyed, the war is lost at that point. A single decisive battle lost can mean the loss of the war. If that is not acceptable, then it should be avoided. Dispersal allows a weaker force to survive damage by a stronger force and attack places less well defended. However, to work the dispersed force must always be in position to attack places left weak or undefended by the strong force. Simply to disperse in a certain area invites piecemeal defeat by the opponent.

As an example, in the American Civil War it would have done no good to disperse conventional Confederate forces in the South to be defeated piecemeal. However, if they dispersed across the North and South or (as actually happened) developed both conventional and unconventional forces, Union forces would have had difficulty trying to be everywhere at once. To fight and win a war against dispersed forces, it is necessary to disperse in such a way that enemy weak points can still be attacked.

The portfolio approach also applies to capabilities. Diversification allows the mixing and matching of capabilities tailoring forces to the needs of the moment. War in the 21st century, as with economics, is very much tied to the need of the moment. Generic, one-size-fits-all capabilities can often mean a shortfall in results or losing out to someone who had the better match of capability to situation. This also is more easily done by insurgents than by conventional armies. Governments and armies have well-established organizations and capabilities that are not easily changed. Witness the battle (since the 1986 Goldwater-Nichols Act) to establish joint war fighting in the U.S. defense establishment as an example. Yet, as we have seen in chapter 2, NGOs are able to add components and capabilities quickly and easily, bringing to bear capabilities tailored to the need of the moment. The diversified portfolio has enormous strength as a strategy.

The diverse portfolio of insurgency needs different ways of organizing. Organizations must function without a hierarchical command structure and be capable of autonomous local action. That is, a given cell in a given area must be capable of performing action without detailed direction from above. Indeed, it is most likely that a given cell in a given area is best equipped to know what it must do and how it should operate. Getting direction from above (beyond general policy and strategy directives) would be useless.

It is possible to engage in insurgency on a wide scale because it does not require concentration of forces to make an attack. As an example, we can note the French Resistance (Maquis) support of the Normandy invasions in World War II. The total number of resistance fighters in France numbered around 70,000, armed primarily with small arms and explosives.[1] Plans were in place for them to attack rail lines (Plan Vert), telephone lines (Plan Violet), and power lines (Plan Bleu) and generally to find ways to waylay German armored reinforcements (Plan Tortue) so they could not get to the Normandy beachhead.[2] Their attacks were highly successful and managed to delay German reinforcements for days or in some cases weeks.[3] Within 24 hours of D Day, some 180 trains had been derailed and 500 rail lines cut.[4] Even regular rail workers took part, shoveling coal off the train so it would run out of coal miles from any refueling station.[5]

The Maquis were organized in small cells of varying size in locations around France. Thousands of fighters were located near population centers and German installations. This was best for gaining intelligence and executing sabotage activity by loosely connected but not centrally commanded forces. Yet, the forces could act as a single unit coordinated in an informal way with Allied command as their actions on D Day proved.

There are many current examples of this. In Chiapas, the Zapatista National Liberation Army (EZLN) organized into cells of 12–16 fighters for sabotage activity.[6] This avoided the risk of decisive battle that government forces were hoping to get to destroy the rebellion. In Chechnya, rebels were organized around clan structures also of 15–20 fighters rather than larger units of organization.[7] These organizations had an overall leadership that connected directly to the fighting organizations with little intervening authority. In contrast, the following is what a traditional but generic hierarchical army organization (from largest to smallest unit) looks like: army, corps, division, brigade, regiment, battalion, company, platoon, squad. There is a good deal of distance between the top leadership and the fighting units. An insurgent organization could mobilize regionally and insert another level command structure, but that seems to be a function of immediate need rather than standard procedure.

Insurgency works by sacrificing concentrated power for speed, surprise, and coverage. Concentrated forces cannot cover all of the places dispersed forces might attack, as seen repeatedly in places like Vietnam or World War II France. Dispersed forces think globally and act locally. That is, they have a general philosophy that all forces follow for fighting the enemy and let that be the guide for their actions locally. They are all generally on the same page in terms of the ultimate goal of their actions, but their actions are all different and more difficult to predict. They sacrifice quantified predictability for wide-scale effect.

The implications for warfare today are important. Global-scale movements (such as Al Qaeda) mean that any target can be hit that is not well defended anywhere insurgents can be sent. That is one of the fundamental problems confronting war planners right now. Conventional forces concentrate to mobilize combat power. That act withdraws control over a wide area, particularly when the mobilization is for offensive action. Offensive action surrenders some of the ability to defend an area, and it makes the rear areas of the conventional force particularly susceptible to attack by infiltration. Conversely, unconventional forces seek local superiority over undefended areas. They flow like water into the cracks in any defense. Conventional forces rely on safe rear areas. Their power is direction oriented. They have vulnerabilities in supply, infrastructure, and communications that are prime targets for unconventional forces.

In the post–cold war era, insurgent movements do not seem to be seeking land or national power in all cases. They seem to be looking for worldwide issue preeminence into which they, and national governments, will fit and live. In other words, they want to remake the world in their image and do it in a way that goes beyond simply overthrowing a single government.

There are other strengths insurgencies have beyond fighting. These strengths lay behind the scenes of what is done on a battlefield. In contrast with national armed forces, insurgencies have lower resource needs. They enjoy an easier and less-formal recruitment and depend on human capabilities rather than technology.

Reconsider the French Resistance example. Notice how various resistance cells were coalesced to fight as a single force all over France on D Day. Both the Allied armies and the Resistance leadership relied on local knowledge provided by the cells living in the operating areas in France. The cells operated in dispersed locations, allowing for greater coverage over all of France. This means some forces inevitably had access to enemy weak points.

This example shows clearly some principles on which insurgency works. Forces have a unifying idea that translates to a goal all work toward rather than a central command structure issuing orders to all units. General rules are developed to avoid being drawn into traps or committing errors. Cells are given local initiative to decide how best they will plan and operate. They rely on communications to get broad command guidance, coordinate timing with other units, report intelligence, and obtain supplies. They need resource backing, which can come from states, other organizations, or criminal organizations, to gain money, training, and weapons.

Fighting against insurgencies is different from fighting conventional forces. The goals and character of war will all be different. The temptation should be resisted to cast it in familiar terms like the Libyan model, by which a government linked to the insurgents is chosen and held responsible for insurgent activity within the country. Most governments in the "war on terrorism" support the United States. If the war continues and all governments are supporting the United States, what will be the next move when more terrorist acts occur?

The solution can only come by changing the way things are done to meet these new challenges. We have to consider how to fight with the diverse portfolio and not overcommit or overspend. Mobilizing a conventional force to chase insurgents through every country on Earth is not a winning strategy. Keep in mind that Al Qaeda (and whichever partners they have) is worldwide. Its supporters and adjuncts are not concentrated, so conventional war is unlikely to produce lasting victory.

Instead, there will be one of two outcomes. Destroying a government will close off some options, but ultimately the effort will grind to a halt without stopping the insurgents. The Taliban has been defeated in Afghanistan, and Al Qaeda is on the run with U.S. forces in pursuit. This is probably not the end of attacks on the United States. Certainly, no one should be planning that way. The second outcome is just as bad. In that scenario, America will need to fight a civil war in every country where the network exists to finally succeed. One outcome gives us no clear victory, the other no clear end and a real risk of world war. It is time to pay more attention to how to fight global insurgency or be left without viable options to protect ourselves in the future.

Defining the Adversary

To counter global insurgency, faster-moving forces are needed. They should be smaller than traditional size units but still numerically superior to those they would face. They should also be ready to fight in a region rather than needing preparation time. The size of the units immediately implies a different, "flatter" command structure than is currently used. Along with this flattened command structure, forces should be able to operate autonomously in a network because they may have to combat a foe who is similarly dispersed. Capabilities also must change their nature. Rather than have capabilities available based on organization, they should be available based on need. Forces may have to change capabilities.

The heart of this global conflict is fighting. Whatever anybody wants to say about bloodless conflicts, new technology, and non-lethal weaponry, warfare is still about fighting and bloodshed. Every war has its own characteristics that separate it from all other wars. It is worthwhile to examine the character of this type of warfare. We need to be able to see its character to be able to defend against it. We can define this character in terms of who, how, and where. In speaking of who, we are talking about what the makeup is of the forces doing the fighting. What is the political organization? To which other groups are they linked? The degree to which we can answer those questions will yield the likelihood of a given group engaging in this type of political violence and what drives them to do it. The question of how is aimed at examining which operations these forces engage in, which techniques of warfare they are using, and by extension, which linkages exist to political goals, what is the size of operations, and for which goals issue organizations are engaging in this type of conflict. The question of where speaks to the battlefields where these conflicts are being fought.

These questions taken in their totality will help us understand why these conflicts are being fought. The specific question of why was discussed in Chapter 2. When we can define the character of the fighting, we will know what needs to be done to engage in this conflict and, to a degree, how to win it. The examination will show us how the fighting is a tool of politics, and it will also lay the groundwork for showing how insurgency is supported.

When we speak of the question of who is doing the fighting, we need to look at the political agendas of the insurgency because they are not fielding large conventional armed forces. Instead, they are arming local groups, with the idea that these local groups will engage in violence on a local level, but their violence will have global consequences.

With this global scope and impact, local political violence reaches a new importance it had not previously attained in the history of warfare.

To know who is doing this, we would have to look at and identify various groups engaging in this type of warfare. We can classify them in a number of different ways using categories established by the Department of State annual report on terrorism: by politics, religion, environment, separatists, or nationalists.[8] There are undoubtedly many more types of groups, but these will suffice at the beginning because these groups have the largest profiles. In fact, groups within these categories already have an established record for political violence.

Religious groups are here quintessentially defined by Al Qaeda, a religious group using violence to further its fundamentalist Moslem message. Environmental groups include the Earth Liberation Front, which has engaged in various types of sabotage of places and things that, in their opinion, harm the environment. Separatist movements include the Chechen guerrillas and the Tamil Tigers, who are seeking to have their own country and previously had been part of another, larger country. There are nationalist groups such as HAMAS (Islamic Resistance Movement), who attempt to advance the cause of a Palestinian homeland and destruction of Israel. These are groups willing to use violence to get what they want. They are also very capable of a low level of the violence, meaning they are not generating large armies and fighting conventional conflicts. Instead, they are generating small groups, scattered in a number of places. Reportedly, Al Qaeda is scattered across 60 to 70 countries. If Al Qaeda cells were all in one nation, they might be large enough to be considered an army (and possibly destroyed by now). Instead, it is comprised of small cells that remain hidden until they are going to perform an action.

We have to note linkages for these groups to understand fully the degree of reach they have and the salience of the issues they are trying to advance. This can be found by looking at the news, by looking on the Web, and by looking at intelligence. In doing this, we try to show who supports the movements and which linkages show adjunct issues, and by extension, we try to show the global coordination and global reach of these groups. In knowing who supports a given group, we can begin to piece together the degree to which common cause brings those groups to collaborate to advance their collective but related agendas. We are looking for the degree to which the issue finds resonance with other people beyond the insurgency's small scope of followers. When we do that, we can also begin to inform ourselves about which issues connect to other issues and the degree to which a given issue, if it is advanced, will also help other issues that are related.

Finally, when we know which groups are willing to support each other and which issues have commonality with each other, we can begin to see the degree to which large groups conform to advance a broad general classification of issues and the degree to which a given group or a constellation of groups is able to generate global coordination of their efforts and global reach for their actions. This is something that Al Qaeda seems to have achieved. There are a number of groups unable to do more than local things, but in concert with the support of Al Qaeda, they are able to advance their local issue as part of a larger global issue constellation, and that is at the heart of what this book is about.

Operations

So, how do these groups fight? To know that, we need to look at the groups discussed and see the operations in which they are engaging. We can already see some general classifications of violence that are used. Obviously, there are suicide bombings, in which a person or persons gather explosives and bring themselves to the midst of a crowd of people, then detonate the bomb, killing themselves and the people surrounding them. Everyone saw what happened on September 11, 2001. It was the largest version of suicide bombing that has been perpetrated on this planet so far and the quintessential illustration of that type of violence.

There is also ambush, in which a group of people waits for a target to pass by and surprise that target, attempting to destroy it with either gunfire or explosives. There is arson, which is violence directed at buildings, symbols, and things of value that are destroyed in the name of political agenda. There is assassination, which actually covers a variety of different types of fighting, including drive-by shootings, surprise executions, and assassinations, such as one sees in movies and on television fairly frequently. There are also kidnappings, which is taking people hostage for ransom, either for money as is done by Abu Sayyaf in the Philippines or in the hopes of gaining a political goal such as the freeing of political prisoners or the withdrawal of occupying troops. Any number of objectives can be fastened to this form of political blackmail.

Conventional bombing also takes place. Conventional bombing is different from suicide bombing in that it is a bomb planted perhaps in a car, perhaps in a suitcase, in an area where people will be and detonated either at a certain time of day or by remote control in the hopes of generating large numbers of casualties or in some cases assassinating political figures. There are also rocket attacks utilizing rocket-propelled grenades or larger rockets with explosives on them to destroy buildings or trucks and tanks or to attack soldiers or civilians in crowded places, generally with heavier weapons than small arms fire.

Note that all of these types of violence are things that require low investment and few participants and are hidden from view in a way that conventional warfare never is. Conventional warfare is known for large standing armies assembled in large bases requiring large sums of money, large stores of material, and information. Here, now, in insurgency a relatively small group of people actually engages in fighting. They do so with less of a "footprint" in terms of finance and material stores, and the operations that they engage in require less coordination because fewer people are taking part in them. It still requires a great deal of support, but the support does not come with the large footprint of the conventional armed force. Instead, even the support is covert and requires less of the population than conventional warfare requires.

It is possible to break insurgencies down by region to see which operations are ongoing in each region, thereby seeing the degree to which violence in each region has its own characteristics and its own variations on this type of war. In Iraq, we see ambush, sabotage, Improvise Explosive Devices (IEDs), rocket attacks, kidnapping, and assassination all taking place amid the backdrop of the recently concluded conventional war that has moved on to insurgency of the type we are examining now. The intensity of what is going on in Iraq lends itself to all options being considered that it are possible to consider on the part of the insurgency in that country.

In the Middle East as a whole, one sees at least on a weekly basis suicide bombs, car bombs, assassinations, and so forth. In the Far East, in places like Indonesia and the Philippines, stories have come to light of kidnappings, bombings (suicide bombings or car bombings), and the like. In the Western Hemisphere, where the violence has a different political flavor to it and is sometimes not only the result of politics but also the result of conflict between governments and organized crime, we also see bombings, ambush, kidnappings, and assassination as well as arson from some of the environmental groups, such as the Earth Liberation Front.

From looking at this violence, we can see some patterns develop on the use of force that will help us understand the practice of violence and the results that the violence generates. The first theme is that no set-piece battles are fought. There is no point at which any of these groups will wish to engage in conflict with conventional forces on a conventional battlefield. Indeed, the whole idea is to avoid facing strengths in short, sharp actions that could result in the destruction of the insurgent force. Instead, the short, sharp actions take place directed at weakness, not against standing armies but against individuals, against population segments, against targets such as nonmilitary buildings and things that are not hardened or well defended.

Confronted with insurgency, an opponent will either contract or disperse to meet this threat. That is, the force will either contract into better defensive positions, as with the strategic hamlet movement in the Vietnam War or its predecessor in Britain's conflict in Malaysia, or an opposing force will disperse and attempt not only to minimize risk but also to come to grips with the insurgent force by breaking itself into smaller pieces and bringing those smaller pieces to bear on the smaller, faster unconventional forces. Either of those two choices will be less effective for the conventional force than fighting a large decisive battle (which may never happen).

The conventional force is built to mass its power together and direct it in one place and time. So, insurgency takes conventional forces out of their comfort zone, that is, their best configuration for utilizing their power. It makes them instead disperse power and attempt either to direct it at a number of places simultaneously (something it is not designed to do) or to cease to use its directed power and instead become a defensive force (something for which it is also not configured). In either case, it becomes easier and more useful for an insurgent force not only to continue the attacks but also to multiply them.

Another aspect of insurgency deals with soft targets, that is, targets with low degrees of survivability and low abilities to defend against violence. These targets have low survivability in the face of violence, particularly surprise violence. The distinction falls along these lines. People, houses, and cars, anything that is not armor plated, surrounded by reinforced concrete, and defendable by large guns or large groups of soldiers, can be considered a soft target. Such targets have no survivability on their own and if they are subject to attack. The only way to defend those targets is with soldiers. Because these soft targets must have people and assets defending them (because they lack their own innate survivability from attack), more resources have to be used in defense, and this begins to spread the available defending assets thinner and thinner. This action also allows the insurgent force to catalog what is defended and select for attack those targets that are not as well defended.

The targets usually chosen are infrastructure, people, or symbols. Targets are chosen for their political significance. Killing large numbers of people who are considered "the enemy" is one form of target.

They also can be political buildings, such as city halls and police stations. Buildings such as the Pentagon and the World Trade Center are not only administrative centers but also symbols of financial and military power that can be selected for destruction.

Attrition is another aspect of insurgency. This is the wearing down of the opposition by numerous attacks over the course of a long period of time rather than one major attack that settles everything in one blow. Again, no set-piece battles are fought. No history-making final conflicts are sought by the insurgent force, no matter how much the conventional forces may want that. Instead, the unconventional force puts together a daily record of small bites: an assassination here, a car bombing there, a kidnapping someplace else. But, every week, even every day, something is done, something that shows to the population that the conventional force and the political machine behind it are less and less able to defend themselves and less and less able to control events, less and less able to win what they think they can win. Insurgency has the effect of wearing down the resolve of even the strongest nations. Because most people do not relish long conflicts, the longer conflict goes on, the more people begin to ask why it has not concluded. There comes a time when so many ask the question that the reasons for the war fade and with it the legitimacy of fighting it. When enough people ask that question, it becomes time to finish a conflict.

Insurgency can be frustrating for even powerful nations. The American government, like many governments, sees its power as a tool to get the things that it wants from the world. But, even with that kind of power there is still a point at which the political rewards of using that power are dependent on the agreement of other people. Because of this, even at the conclusion of a conventional conflict if the defeated people do not deliver their agreement, or at least their acquiescence, to yield to the victorious army, then the rewards of power are delayed. The deferment of those rewards in the short term can be detrimental; the longer that deferment continues, the more possible it is that the rewards will never happen.

This is what is going on in Iraq right now. The longer the deferment continues, the more people begin to question whether it was worth expending the effort. Those who are either inclined to disagree with power or are in opposition to power will also begin to question why they need to reward power, another part of what is going on Iraq right now. Indeed, that is what is going on around the world. Many people in many places have absorbed the lesson of the last 60 years that in a conventional war few can stand against America, and some of them (Vietnam, Lebanon, Somalia, Iraq) adopted the course of insurgency. They recognized that, ultimately, no matter how great, the power rewards of the use of that power must come by agreement no matter how much force is used.

Insurgencies require less investment. Insurgencies do not require a large standing army or the type of logistics that goes with it. It does not require a large bureaucracy to generate new weapons and new technology and administer personnel. Indeed, this type of warfare requires things that are low technology and low cost. If one wanted to destroy the World Trade Center, it could be done with a submarine firing cruise missiles, and that would be effective. It would take a number of cruise missiles to do the job, and by extension it would take a large amount of money and technological investment to build the submarine. It would take money to develop the technology for the submarine to do what it does. It would take a large investment to generate the cruise missile. Instead, the perpetrators of that act decided that they would simply hijack planes and use them as cruise missiles. So, for the price of plane tickets men with box cutters took over four planes and turned them into cruise missiles. Low technology and low cost are the hallmarks of this type of warfare.

Insurgent warfare requires relatively few people to do a great deal of damage with these types of attack. Let us return to the example of a submarine launching cruise missiles at the World Trade Center. The submarine would probably have a crew of 100 or so. If the American Navy knew where to find it and destroy it before or after it unleashes its attack, then that would still be the loss of 100 people and the attending value of the submarine and its technology. Contrast this to the destruction that was wrought on September 11, 2001. Over 3,000 people were killed for the lives of 19 men. If that were a conventional conflict, it would be an unmitigated catastrophe for whoever lost 3,000 people. So, for the loss of relatively a few insurgents, a great deal of damage was done, which maximizes the costs of engaging in the violence in a way that conventional warfare does not. Conventional warfare may not be able to keep up, relatively speaking, with unconventional warfare in terms of cost for the operation versus damage or "bang for the buck."

There is also no timetable associated with this type of warfare. In conventional warfare, there is always a timetable associated with action, an operations tempo by which forces who have to be on alert can only be on alert for a certain time before they begin to lose their effectiveness, and forces in the field must be brought out of the field on occasion and given rest and refitting to maintain their effectiveness. That places a limit on the timing of operations (as we see in Iraq). Yet, with unconventional warfare, these considerations are not as important. Forces dispersed in the field or wherever they are dispersed can stay dispersed for long periods of time. They are not supported by a large logistical machine. Many are leading the lives of ordinary citizens, supporting themselves with jobs and waiting for the day when they will do what it is they have come to do.

These forces require no assembly. A conventional force, before it goes to war, must have a time and place to assemble because its effectiveness rests on its ability to mass. It must have a place where forces can mass and be sure that those forces are correctly armed and provisioned before they can move into battle as a larger force. The larger the operation, the more time and the larger the place needed to assemble.

By contrast, an insurgent force lives by dispersion. It must stay dispersed to survive, so this force will not need to assemble. It is probably already living in the area where it is going to operate. Because it requires much less in terms of logistics, it is not necessary for the force to assemble to provision or to fight. It requires very little in the way of provisions, so the provisions can be delivered covertly. It also requires little in the way of transportation. Above all, it requires no uniformity. Each dispersed small group is given money to gather what it needs to be able to fight, and that changes from place to place.

Conventional armed forces require uniformity, and that uniformity can be a great advantage in the field, but globally it can be a disadvantage because that uniformity means that some piece of what it normally uses for operations will not be relevant to wherever they are fighting. It takes even more time to acclimate people and equipment to a given place in a way the people already living there have already done.

A global insurgent warfare force is facilitated in all these ways. Its global logistics is much smaller and in its own way as effective as the logistics of conventional forces. This allows it to move faster and be more acclimated to its conditions than the conventional force. To do this, the insurgent force sacrifices power. It has no power to take over a country and has no power to take over the planet in and of itself. But, as long as it champions an idea and survives, the possibility exists that more and more people will also champion the idea. If enough people flock to the idea, it stands a chance of winning acceptance in more parts of the world, making the movement more powerful.

New Battlefields

Where are these conflicts being fought? Currently, they are being fought in cities and in ports rather than on battlefields. Indeed, in recent times there have been very few formal battlefields. It has been quite some time since we have seen a battle like Austerlitz, Gettysburg, or Normandy, in part because warfare has been pulled toward insurgency, and insurgents do not mass. Because they appear as regular citizens until they unleash their violence, we do not see them on battlefields. Instead, we see them undercover as ordinary people living ordinary lives; in the 21st century, this means primarily that they live and work in cities and in ports.

This is not just because no set-piece battles are being fought. Guerrilla warfare was often fought in rural areas in the past. In the rural areas, they would have a base considered safe from attack by way of distance and lack of access for conventional force. Now, these unconventional forces have moved into cities. That is where they choose to operate, so that is where the conventional forces must go to find them, whether they want to or not.

Part of the reason for operating in cities is that insurgent forces do not concentrate in one place, or they can be scattered across a large city or many minor cities. Also, insurgent operations and support seem better suited in the 21st century to cities. Cities are also political centers because they attract large numbers of people to live there, which also makes it better for insurgent forces to hide in those places. The political aspects of cities and ports are many. Targets with political value are primarily in cities. Political figures live in cities. Municipal buildings are in cities. If politics dictates that the insurgency is being fought against foreigners, foreigners will primarily be found in cities.

People are also moving more and more into cities, and that provides the insurgent force with a number of useful things.[9] People provide an audience. Carrying out war in the countryside means that most people will not see it and will be less affected by the violence as a result. People who are eyewitnesses to war, on the other hand, are bound to have very strong feelings one way or the other. Engaging in operations in a city in front of the city's population makes certain that everyone in a city knows that this conflict is taking place. It forces them to make up their minds about it. By extension, having operations in a city where a large population is centered makes it easier to recruit people. Because people primarily live more and more in cities, they are neighbors to the participants in conflict, and this means that it is much easier to recruit new members in a city than it ever was in a rural area.

People also offer camouflage. If an unconventional warfare group is operating in a city and they are using the cover of being ordinary people within the everyday population of the city, then they are simply part of the daily increase of the population of many cities around the world. It might be easy to find insurgents in a small town with a population of 500 or fewer and where the terrorists are new to the city. In such a place, it will be a giveaway if people do not know them, and on their arrival terrorist activities begin. In large population centers, it is very difficult to distinguish one face in 1,000 or 10,000 or 1 million who might or might not be operating as part of an insurgent force. Because of this, it is highly desirable to be able to operate within a city where before, during, and even after an operation, hiding is a simple matter of acting like everyone else—a face amid a sea of faces.

Finally, there is a support aspect to consider. In a rural area, it is very difficult to get new supplies. If the insurgent forces need explosives, weapons, ammunition, or medical supplies, they ultimately risk being caught because they had those supplies brought to them by someone from the outside. Or, just as conspicuously, they must infiltrate a city to get those things. But, if the force already resides within the city, it becomes much easier to go to a store someplace. Even black market connections are a possibility to gather ammunition, food, and medical supplies, and in some societies there will be nothing conspicuous about gathering any of those things within a city.

It is also easier to connect to the outside world through a city than in rural areas. Among the many things that are headquartered in large cities are the media, not only state-run media, but also world media. If conflict is going on in a given city, the world news media will descend on it and cover the story, and it is much easier for them to cover that story if it is happening inside a city rather than in some rural area they may or may not be able to reach. It is not just the media that provide the connection. Modern cities are also communications hubs. They contain the places where transportation junctures such as railroads, highways, and airports as well as seaports convene. They are also places where phone lines and radio and TV station towers are located. This allows access by way of the Internet to the world in a way that is less possible in rural areas.

Finance is more feasible in cities because they are centers of finance. Money runs through cities. Banks are in cities. Jobs are in cities. Investment happens in cities. So, it is possible for funding to be sent electronically to a bank account at a bank in a city where the insurgents have only to go to an ATM machine to get their funding. Contrast this with living in rural areas, where money must be acquired in cash from outside.

Operations are also easier within a city. Cities are good places to hide. As stated, everyone is part of a sea of faces. This makes it easier to stay under cover before the operation and easy to disappear after the operation. It is easier to use secrecy and camouflage in a city if the operation takes place there than it would be to attempt to gain entry to a city from outside.

The geography of a city favors smaller units. Older cities are set up with narrow streets, relatively speaking to rural areas, and the confines of cities mean that large units must necessarily split up because there is not enough room for large numbers of units to accumulate in one place. Because of this, the massing of combat power is much more problematical in a city for a conventional force than it would be in a rural area where there are wide open spaces. The lessened effectiveness comes from units being broken down into smaller pieces. They will be faster, but at a cost to firepower and the safety provided by larger numbers. with less combat power, which means that it is possible for the smaller units to be isolated and overwhelmed by the unconventional warfare forces within a city. This will not happen all of the time to be sure, but should be when the occasion presents itself.

The amount of automobile or foot traffic in a city also slows conventional warfare forces. Even in the midst of a Stalingrad-style operation, where the city is destroyed in the battle, there will be people living in a city who are going to be moving in the places where operations take place. Whether the conventional force is there to protect the people or to destroy the people, those people become a hindrance to conventional operations in a city; this also gives benefit to the insurgency, which for its own preservation is counting above all on being quicker and more secret than the conventional force.

This problem is made more acute by the fact that the conventional warfare force is relying on maps to navigate the city; in many cases, those maps do not show accurate details of the city's composition. They will not show traffic patterns, construction, or debris; this will also hinder the conventional force.

Related to this problem is the problem of native intelligence. People who are living within a city have better access to what is going on in the city than a conventional force who lives sequestered within or outside a city ever will. This means that they will know more about what is going on, and they will have as good or better idea of how people feel about what is going on in a city as the conventional forces will. They will be better able to engage in counterintelligence and disinformation within a city because they will be able to do it directly by word of mouth. An insurgent force who has been living within a city can get to know the city very well. They can learn something that conventional warfare forces probably cannot do easily, which is engaging in off-road navigation. When living in a place, it becomes possible at some point to be able to get to a destination without reference to the road system. Young children all over the world learn whose yard they can cut through to get where they want go, and that information is very important because people who have never been to a city will navigate on main roads. That will fairly hinder their ability to defend themselves or engage in offensive operations as a result. People who do understand how to get around in a city without reference to the roads will be able to move faster on either attack or defense.

City geography favors the operations discussed at the beginning of this chapter: ambush, car bombs, suicide bombs, and kidnappings. These operations are easy to do because they happen faster, and their targets are primarily people. It is easy to engage in an operation and then disappear because the targets are people and the people are in cities. Living amid the targets of operations, there is no need for assembling large forces and traveling to the objective in force. This is an enormous advantage compared with conventional forces, who still must assemble and travel to the area where it will fight. Indeed, they may have to fight their way through to the area where operations will take place.

Arms can be procured and then more easily hidden within cities, and the illustration of that fact is the degree to which criminals in Western countries can obtain weapons readily and easily no matter how much the police departments of the world attempt to stop them. Because the police can never get all the weapons off the streets, the indication is that it will be easier in other places for insurgents to obtain weaponry and use it. Indeed, cities represent commerce centers, so there will be ports of entry of one kind or another for bringing in all manner of weapons and ammunition in addition to new stocks of food every week, depending on the city, and new chemicals that can be used for explosives. Communications support is better and easier to get within cities. This includes the media, which no longer have to travel to the theater of operations. The theater of operations is right in front of them.

Warfare Redefined

Warfare is being pulled in a completely different direction from the strengths of conventional forces and how they operate. The warfare that we have seen over the last 10 years has been moving inexorably in the direction of insurgency in cities. Conventional forces were not built or trained to engage in this type of warfare, and it is not something for which they can reconfigure themselves overnight. Indeed, it is not clear that they should be fully reconfigured for this because it is not clear whether there will never be conventional wars ever again.

An offshoot of this type of warfare is that high-technology machinery and precision-guided munitions have become less useful. If the fighting that is going on is taking place inside a city, then precision-guided missiles, cruise missiles, and the like may not be very useful, especially if the politics of the conflict preclude doing a large amount of damage to a city or its population. Because the fighting is taking place inside the city and it is not conventional fighting, the various sensors that are being used are designed for the conventional battlefield. As a result, the urban battlefield may not yield results in the types of signal intelligence on which conventional forces rely. Although such intelligence may be very useful for warning, tracking, and listening in on a conventional armed force, it may not be as useful in an urban setting, where potential opponents live next to each other and can talk to each other on the front steps.

There is no traditional mass and maneuver going on in urban-based insurgency. This type of warfare is much more about dispersal and watchfulness than it ever was about massing forces, consolidating inside a city, and moving forward against an opponent who has done something similar. We are not talking about Stalingrad. Each side will be brought to fight among their friends and live among their enemies in a way that conventional warfare never required.

This kind of warfare strips away many of the advantages that accrue to conventional armed forces compared to conventional war. Indeed, it can be said that the art of war was not invented so that the strong may conquer. It was invented so that the weak may contend with the strong. That is an overall theme and rationale for the migration of fighting into cities. Cities strip away the advantages that the strong have and give new advantages to those previously considered the weak.

Global insurgency makes it possible for various local movements to be global without being conventional. If there is a given faction in every major city on the continent and that faction is able to engage in insurgency anywhere on the continent, it possesses global power. It relies on like-minded people scattered in various places to act in concert nationwide or worldwide. Insurgent operations need less care and feeding to be successful. Because of that, it is easier for ordinary people to do it. Access makes it possible. Access to weapons, access to technology, and access to communications facilitate ordinary people engaging in insurgency and being effective against conventional forces. As advantages are stripped away from conventional forces, power is given to or acquired by the ordinary people engaging in insurgency. In taking warfare away from its conventional form, insurgents change it. Because it is global insurgency, it allows their politics to be global also.

Chapter 4

INTELLIGENCE

The work of collection, analysis, and production of intelligence used to belong only to governments. Only governments had money and authority to collect information on others, usually other governments that were rivals for power in some way. The need for intelligence was driven by national security concerns, such as who was building a powerful army or new battleships. These requirements drove intelligence to develop (for powerful nations) into an ability to find out what was being built, in what quantities, and for what effects. Intentions, although also important, slowly took a back seat during the cold war to the more technical aspects of intelligence connected to the arms race. This was acceptable in those days because there were far fewer decision makers, only a relative handful of nations instead of nearly 200. Because nearly all major decision makers until the 1990s were from governments, the intelligence apparatus was government owned and parochial.

Now, in addition to nation states, nonstate actors and multinational corporations have intelligence needs. This makes intelligence a market-driven commodity. Anyone who can produce intelligence can sell it to whoever wants to buy it. This is not the same intelligence governments get, although arguably it can be better. Intelligence can be used to support decisions in a variety of situations beyond national security. Corporations or nongovernmental organizations (NGOs) can require intelligence in situations that can be violent but do not present threats from other nations. Government intelligence also has variety, but no one outside government has access to it.

Nonstate actors need access to intelligence, and their needs require collection, research, and analysis tailored to their focus. Yet, for the same reasons they do not concentrate physically in the same place, they do not field the same formal intelligence apparatus as governments. It is expensive to build an intelligence community to support decision making. The nations of the world spend billions of dollars on it each year. But, other people and organizations also produce intelligence, and customers may pay for the product without paying for the apparatus that produced it. A need is served not only to nations but also to large companies and nonstate actors. Anyone with an intelligence requirement can get it. That is how consumer intelligence is born.

Collection can come from a number of sources (many unsophisticated), like coast watchers, spies, stooges, social engineering, hacking, commercial satellites, and so on. Spy novels tend to picture intelligence collection as sophisticated, and it can be, but it does not have to be. Before the 20th century, intelligence was collected by people seeing, hearing, and stealing things and reporting them to those who required the information. This type of collection is relatively easy to field by consumer firms, by the organizations themselves, or even by the average human being. This collection will not be as sophisticated and exacting as, say, U.S. intelligence collection. It also will not be as expensive because the assets are contracted, not built. In fact, collection can be done by a combination of nonstate agents and contract operatives more cheaply than building and launching satellites or setting up listening posts. This is made easier with cell phones, computers, and digital photography. Imagine an operative with a digital camera and a cell phone taking a picture of something, notifying a client that there is intelligence for sale, and sending it by e-mail in return for a fee. It can be just that easy.

Think of this hypothetical scenario: Al Qaeda is notified by collaborators placed in the governments of nations situated between Yemen and the United States that the *U.S.S. Cole* is going to Yemen. From these collaborators, Al Qaeda knows the approximate day of the *Cole*'s arrival in Yemen for refueling. Coast watchers with cell phones, planted on the coasts of nations along the way or in boats, phone in sightings of the *Cole*. More watchers on the Red Sea pinpoint the arrival time and location of the *Cole*'s final approach to Yemen. The bombers are then notified to activate and launch their successful attack. This is done largely with human intelligence (HUMINT). It is not known whether this is really how the *Cole* was tracked and attacked, but it is certainly plausible and shows that it can be done without great cost and sophistication.

Information in raw form does not help decision making. It must be researched, processed, and analyzed to be useful. Analysis marries data collection to research to produce useful information. This research can be done in libraries and on the Internet by developing a background picture of the area of interest. The research sets up a backdrop to direct collection focus and develop context to understand the collected information. Much can be found on the Internet. Papers are posted on the Internet by academic experts. Many professional journals have a Web site with an archive section. Web sites on the target focus may exist. They may not give specifics, but they will give background and show where to focus collection to fill in the holes. The Internet has made research accessible to anyone.

Analysis completes the intelligence picture by marrying collection to background research for decision support. The product that comes from analysis will show varying accuracy depending on proficiency in these three components. Analysis helps define options and make predictions about choices and risk. In the cold war this was a specialized field. Now, political risk analysis agencies are springing up to assist private companies in consumer intelligence analysis. They analyze the risk of taking actions (like insurance and investment) in political contexts.

There is a relative advantage to this type of intelligence. It is market and issue driven and therefore easier to refocus to more timely topics. Because it must serve varying clients, it is more difficult to fall into traps of single proficiency in a narrow area. Thus, where the U.S. intelligence community had trouble figuring out what its focus should be after the cold war, consumer-driven intelligence cannot focus on a single subject, particularly if it has a diversified client base.

Government intelligence, particularly in the United States, is technology heavy to support locating targets and keeping track of other nations' physical assets and infrastructure. It watches other governments, usually by satellite or eavesdropping measures. There is great value in this type of intelligence. However, it is good at producing numbers (usually of ships, aircraft, tanks, missiles, etc.) but not intentions. Thus, it has a shortcoming that has proved more than once to be a hole in the U.S. intelligence picture. Bureaucracy-driven intelligence counts on long lead time for warning. Against a large conventional force (like the former Soviet Army), the lead time is not a big problem because large armies take a long time to assemble and move. However, against more fast-moving opponents such as guerillas and drug smugglers, the lead time is a great hindrance.

Consumer intelligence is more reliant on HUMINT. Human beings go to the places for which intelligence is required and learn of what is going on. This is necessary for predicting consequences of various actions. In many cases, it is better to get information from experts who have investigated things with their own eyes than through intercepted signals.

In the push and pull of intelligence production, nonstate actors have the advantage of a low profile compared to governments. They have less overhead in terms of buildings and installations that need to be defended, hidden, or even populated. Conversely, governments possess targets that are well known. Those targets not only are military, but also can be financial or cultural. Nonstate actors are less vulnerable to that. Much of their capital is philosophical and intellectual, and their infrastructure is flexible and much more easily rebuilt.

Ad hoc issue-based organizations/groups may bring diverse expertise and ability to bear on a problem. As more organizations join together, they add their distinctiveness, experience, and expertise to the network. They can develop analysis and collection tailored to the occurring situation. Nonstate actor intelligence can disband and reconfigure or reconstitute quicker than government intelligence can. This "amateur" intelligence is less awe inspiring, but it gives nonstate actors the chance to engage in coordinated global activity. Anyone who doubts this need look no further than the September 11th attacks for verification.

Intelligence is a strange animal. We are led to believe that it is difficult, complex, expensive, and technology driven. It is all of those things in its most professional form as practiced, for example, by the Central Intelligence Agency (CIA). It has big budgets, satellites, and eavesdropping capabilities. The less-well-known thing is that intelligence can still be effective when it is not in its most professional form. An underlying theme of this book is that simply being effective works, and nonprofessionals can achieve that effectiveness. To understand why it works, we must see what intelligence does at various levels.

Intelligence provides information to help decision makers decide what to do, how to do it, when to do it, and which threats are out there. Large military operations, like the Normandy invasion, Desert Storm, or Iraqi Freedom require something like a CIA and everything it can offer. Smaller operations can live with less-sophisticated means. Smaller operations need more local intelligence relevant to a smaller group. Technology is nice, but it is not the only way to go to be effective.

Intelligence has been gathered effectively for centuries without technology. It has been done usually by way of human observation and commonsense extrapolation of those observations. The basic equation looks like this: Take what was seen; decide what it means and how it can be used. Observation is the still a key to intelligence gathering and is simple enough for anyone to use.

For instance, in World War II the Allies used coast watchers and the British Royal Observer Corps to watch for the enemy. The job of the coast watchers in the South Pacific was simply watching Japanese ships sailing by various islands in the Pacific, noting the passage of those ships, and reporting them to higher command. The Royal Observers were an integral part of the defense of Britain during the Battle of Britain. Once aircraft passed over the British coast, radar was no longer effective because it only pointed outward from the coast. At that point, only the Royal Observer Corps was able to keep track of German planes coming in and to radio the positions of the planes to higher command so that decisions could be made. Simple human observation is an exceptionally effective means of gathering intelligence to be used by decision makers.

There is an implication to this idea. The most professional form of intelligence as practiced by the CIA and other government agencies works for large-scale, conventional warfare operations. The lesser form may be just as useful for smaller-scale operations. In large operations, there is a need to know where the enemy is, in what numbers, and with what capabilities. In wars between nations, particularly large nations, these questions and answers delve into some fairly large-scale information collection. In this type of collection, the capabilities often equal the threat. Few ideas on intentions in the minds of decision makers are necessarily gathered. This is done through other means. Simply recording the numbers and capabilities of an opposing force is complex and happens on a large scale but is inherently simple compared to figuring out intentions. This kind of large-scale intelligence is not really built to find those things out.

We now find ourselves faced with insurgency warfare, and the sort of intelligence that we are describing here as the most professional form of intelligence is oriented to bringing two national armies to have a battle. As such, it is geared to finding out where the enemy is, in what numbers, and with what capabilities. On the other hand, in insurgency warfare large-scale conventional forces are not always seen, and the object is often to avoid conventional large-scale battle. Locating an individual like Osama bin Laden proves difficult without good human intelligence (HUMINT). The problem becomes even more difficult if the subject (as with bin Laden) withdraws from using technology to avoid being tracked.

Finding out plans, intentions, and timing is more important in insurgency. Because small-scale operations can have large-scale results, this becomes exceptionally important. Keep in mind that the attacks on the World Trade Center and the Pentagon on September 11 were devastating and perpetrated by just 19 people. It is possible for an operation that exists on a fairly small scale to have disproportionately destructive results. Yet, because it is a small-scale operation, it cannot be tracked using processes used in the most professional form of intelligence for tracking the conventional armed forces. When fighting an insurgency war (on either side), intelligence effectiveness is much more a question of knowing intentions and timing than it is knowing capabilities and numbers.

Ordinary people can and do gather intelligence for their own decisions. This happens every day for anything from buying groceries, to buying a car, to buying a house. They can even gather intelligence the way professionals do but on a much lower level. Keep in mind they only have to be effective, not astounding. It is often only required that a certain degree of accuracy (which does not have to be 100% accurate) is necessary to succeed. The tools to be effective are now accessible to anyone.

We can show the implications of this sort of "low-intensity" intelligence gathering, which we anticipate here and now as the following: They do not have to gather secret military information. The targets are usually open and accessible to the public and are civilian in nature. They require much less sophistication to be effective.

To understand these things better, we can create a template for intelligence like professionals do. The template is simple and consists of these steps: direction, collection, analysis and production, and dissemination. We can look at each of these things and see which tools are available for amateurs to mimic the professionals. To help our understanding, we can see examples of how people have done these things. In this way, we can paint a picture that it is possible for amateurs to gather effective intelligence to support their operations in a way that approximates what professionals do in support of governments and their armed forces.

We can build our template for describing amateur intelligence by looking at how the professionals do it. A glance at the CIA Web site provides a good starting point. As we begin, let us proceed with this caveat. It is important not to equate amateurs and professionals. That is not what is intended in this chapter. The message is not that what amateurs do or could do is as good or better than what the CIA does. We are simply noting that, in the right context, amateurs can be effective, and that is all that is needed. In other words, the CIA has enormous resources at its command and is capable of finding out many of the things, if not all of the things, that it wants to know. Even then, intelligence agencies are still at the mercy of whoever is asking for information as to whether it is being directed to the right place, among many other problems that intelligence agencies have historically had.

However, the CIA stands at the top of the pantheon of intelligence gatherers, along with a few other national governments in the world. We are not equating amateur collectors of intelligence with them. What we are saying, instead, is that if the targets are simpler and the operations are simpler, professional-level intelligence gathering may not be required to achieve objectives and be effective. It may only be necessary to gather some of what national intelligence agencies might gather, and that information may be readily and easily accessible to the average human being.

We can define the rudimentary intelligence capability the same way the CIA does with these steps[1]:

- *Direction and Planning*: Deciding what information is needed to support various types of plans and decisions.
- *Collection*: Finding the information necessary to the decision-making process.
- *Analysis and Production*: Taking the collected information and making it legible and relevant.
- *Dissemination*: Delivering the relevant information to the targeted user.

Direction and Planning

When a plan is made, information is needed, and the need becomes intelligence requirements. Intelligence requirements fuel intelligence planning and the direction of intelligence collection. These requirements go from the general to the specific, from the decision maker to the executing agent. Decision makers not only can be leaders of nations such as presidents, generals, and prime ministers but also can be leaders of organizations or corporations. These decision makers need intelligence on possible directions for action that supports their agenda. This may include intelligence on a political climate of a particular place in which they are interested. It may also include expected reactions to various types of action that could take place in a given area of operations they have selected. It could also be a scouting report on potential targets in the selected area.

Beneath that level, there are planners. These planners attempt to fulfill the direction of higher authority as they request action to satisfy the political agendas that have been set. These planners need to know information about the targets selected for operations. This is more specific information than that requested by high-level decision makers. For instance, they could require information on the features of a given town in terms of bridges, buildings, shipping, or train traffic that may prove to be good targets for operations. Targeting those features requires information. Information is needed to help make decisions on the most effective actions on to take on these targets. This leads to questions about resources needed to support those actions. Even as that is being investigated, it is also necessary to discover what the most effective time for a prospective action might be. Logistics becomes a consideration in terms of gathering and transporting resources in support of the people who will carry out the operation.

Finally, the people executing the action have their own needs. They need more details about the targets against which they will operate and more specifics about what those targets are and what their characteristics might be. They need information that will help them decide which actions will be most effective and in what timing to fulfill their operational tasks. They need to know how to gain access to those targets. They need to know what is needed to keep things secret until the time of the operation. They also must know which threats exist with potential to stop the actions they intend to take.

Overall, we can generalize that these types of information need to be collected: targets from the general to the specific, resources, logistics, tasks, secrecy, threats, timing, and access. With the requirements in hand, intelligence collectors can begin to flesh out more specifically what information they need to collect. The problem then becomes how to find it and where.

Collection

The requirements of collection are complex and interrelated. How can amateurs engage in collection of the previously defined requirements effectively? The answer is in the venues discussed in Chapters 1–3. Gathering intelligence on military and government people and places is difficult. Those people and places reside or work in restricted locations, and the information in their charge tends to be well guarded. However, gathering information on public places and the people working in those public places is much less difficult. Those places are accessible to the largest portion of the population, and they are less well guarded. Gathering information on unprotected places and people is easier still. The reason is that these targets are among us, and we all have and need access to them to keep civilization moving. As long as the targets of operations are not secret military installations, it is very possible for amateurs to collect relevant intelligence for insurgent operations.

How can this intelligence be collected? To answer this, we can return to the CIA Web site, which describes various types of intelligence it collects. Note that the more types of intelligence one can use, the more accurate the overall picture becomes. We can select from those types the ones that are most possible for amateurs to use because they are available not only to national governments but also to anyone. Our selection includes[2]

- OSINT: open source intelligence
- HUMINT: human intelligence
- IMINT: imagery intelligence
- SIGINT: signal intelligence

As this exploration goes forward, it will be necessary to distinguish between some things. Government intelligence agencies are sanctioned to gather intelligence; amateurs are not. As such, we must also distinguish between legal and illegal means of intelligence collection. Much of the intelligence gathering we discuss here is considered illegal for engagement by private citizens. Indeed, professionals gather intelligence, placing themselves in danger of prison or death in the process. That is a constant worldwide that must be kept in mind as it underscores the seriousness of intelligence gathering.

Open Source Intelligence

Open source intelligence comes from information available to anyone.[3] It can come from books in libraries, news stories, and Web sites. Sources must still be credible. Rumors must be filtered. It is possible to produce a wealth of information on any subject using OSINT. It is the start of a larger research project. Research here shows which questions remain unanswered. OSINT shows what we can know right now and points us in the direction of what we still need to know that must be obtained through other means. Other forms of intelligence are then used to fill those holes. OSINT is probably the most common source of intelligence gathering.

OSINT is not always benign. It is possible for intelligence products to be classified even though the information from which those products are created is not classified. Information leads to conclusions. Connecting the dots the right way leads to conclusions that are much more important than the information those conclusions are derived. As an example, note the "Phoenix memo" in which a Federal Bureau of Investigation agent called attention to the fact that people suspected of being Al Qaeda operatives were taking lessons in how to fly.[4] The information in and of itself did not seem as important to everyone before September 11 as it did afterward. In retrospect, that information and other information that seemed benign were quite powerful when taken together in the right context.

Plenty of organizations beyond the CIA gather intelligence. It is possible to be effective and competent without being a professional government agency. There is a story of a competition that was held by a U.S. Air Force general among intelligence agencies, both government and private and including the CIA . The object for the contestants was to come up with the most complete report on the nation of Burundi in Africa. Each contestant was allowed to use whatever tools they had at their disposal to find out everything they could in a certain time period. Interestingly, the CIA lost. The winning contestant was a private company, Open Source Solutions. In just 2 days, Open Source Solutions came up with what was judged the most complete report using open sources alone and won the competition.[5] The implications of this tale are meant to reinforce the point of this chapter, and this book; namely, intelligence gathering, like warfare, is no longer a monopoly of governments.

Obviously, there are limits to what OSINT can accomplish. One can produce a detailed general report but probably not a foreign minister's itinerary based on OSINT. That said, it may not always be necessary to have those types of details if the objective is to support the types of operations discussed in Chapter 3.

In recent years, companies have begun to generate OSINT to compete with each other. This is not new as companies have been practicing industrial espionage across the 20th century, but more formalized, open-source competitive intelligence capabilities are being produced by companies in the 21st century as a means of informing decision making and forecasting the future. As an example, we can note the work of Leonard Fuld in the field of competitive intelligence, as it is called. Fuld consults with companies on the need for competitive intelligence and helps them develop those capabilities. The object is to try to forecast the future or know the present and plan accordingly using open source information.[6]

Obviously, groups like Al Qaeda can, and probably do, collect intelligence this way to know political climates, for instance. Average folks do this each time they go to a Web site like MapQuest or Google. We all seek information to inform current decisions and future plans.

Since September 11, that has become more difficult as people have begun to remove information on possible targets and locations from their Web sites. Reportedly, the Department of Energy used to carry maps of locations of their nuclear facilities on its Web site.[7] There have been Web sites that allow people to locate a residence by punching in a phone number.[8] People are slowly becoming aware of the possible danger of sensitive information that used to be open information being on the Internet and the damage that information can cause. Some are being more careful; others are not. There has not been any talk about illegal means of gathering OSINT because, by definition, OSINT is open to all. By itself, it is an effective means to learn a subject and directs further inquiries using other means.

Human Intelligence

Human intelligence is probably the oldest form of intelligence gathering. It consists of simple human observation.[9] From HUMINT, one learns to ask these questions: Where did you go? What did you see? What did you hear? To whom did you talk? Asking someone to collect that information is fairly simple provided you can obtain the information from the person who is gathering it. Because most people will become suspicious at openly answering these questions about themselves, HUMINT must be gathered in secret. That points to the difficulty of HUMINT: getting the information from the person gathering it. This can be difficult if the collector must maintain secrecy and avoid being caught by anyone. The information source is renewable. This means one can keep asking new questions and getting new information from the HUMINT resource unless that resource gets caught.

HUMINT can be simple or complex. It can be done by professionals or amateurs, depending on what is needed. At its simplest, HUMINT may be a person standing on a street corner counting cars as they go by. At its most complex, it may be infiltrating the inner circle of a powerful leader and finding out that leader's habits and intentions. The simplest HUMINT can be done by any of us. The most complex intelligence takes great training and attention to detail as well as resources. Bear in mind that targets now are not necessarily military or government installations. Targets and operations discussed in Chapters 1–3 point to things average people can go to and observe.

It has been easier in the past to generate HUMINT capabilities to spy on nearby (and more familiar) places. It is much harder to generate those capabilities and send the people to a distant (and less familiar) place. The reason for this is that, to be effective in gathering

HUMINT, the collector must be able to blend in to the surroundings and be indistinguishable from the population in which they operate. This means that to send someone to someplace else, it would be necessary to train that person to do that type of blending in. It is easier for someone to do that when sending a person to the United States because there are so many cultures in the United States, and so many people come here from so many different countries all the time that it would be easy enough simply to send someone without training them to blend in. At the same time, it has probably been quite difficult for American intelligence to find people to send to countries in the Eastern Hemisphere to blend in unless they recently immigrated from other nations. Many nations are more homogeneous, and its citizens more easily recognize outsiders. Another solution is to find someone in the area where you want to gather the HUMINT that supports you and your cause well enough and ask him or her to commit what would be considered treason against the country in which they live. That is not unheard of, and many countries do it.

HUMINT requires reliable observers and people with common sense. They must be quiet and unobtrusive, not at all like James Bond or other Hollywood-style secret agents. They must be people who suggest nothing to anyone who observes them. They must be people who are not easily described and have few distinguishing characteristics. They must be people who disappear quickly from memory. They must move quickly and easily among people and make their observations, and nobody really remembers that they were there or what they were doing. They are simply private citizens walking around observing what goes on.

There are legal and illegal aspects to HUMINT. Part of the legal-versus-illegal argument has to do with the intent of the observation. We engage in legal HUMINT when we go to see if something we want is on sale or get out of our cars amid a traffic jam to see what has caused it. It is legal because it is benign. HUMINT becomes illegal when someone decides to observe a bridge to judge how best to destroy it. There is a gray area in all of this, and it has to do with gathering information people would not want you to know but is available, such as the ability to buy driver's license information. For many years, it has been possible for people to do that, yet most people would not want the information on their driver's license available to just anyone. It is not clear where the legalities fall, and it is still being decided in appeals courts. Thus far, court decisions have tended to favor people at least having the option to say that they prefer not to have their information on their driver's license sold to private companies.

There are a few ways we can break down HUMINT usefully. We can start with observations. Observations look at locations, traffic, behavior, and documents. HUMINT also encompasses listening. Observers mingle with people and listen to their conversations. This has been done effectively in the past, as evidenced by Nazi Germany's infiltration of the New York waterfront during World War II, which led to a number of ships sunk by German U-boats. As a result, at some point it became necessary to warn people not to talk out loud about sensitive information such as ship arrival and departure times, hence the saying "loose lips sink ships."

HUMINT also encompasses asking questions. Collectors talk to people and find out what they think about certain things, what their reactions are to certain topics, and what yearnings they have materially, spiritually, or politically. This information can serve any level of decision making, from political through operational. It all depends on the need of the decision makers and the actions they are attempting to execute.

A more illustrative story comes from the wars in Chechnya. A Chechen leader was charged with gathering intelligence on the Russians occupying Chechnya and using HUMINT in a number of ways. He contacted friends and relatives in occupied territories, with no orders except to observe the Russians comings and goings. They were simply to be private citizens. They were instructed to walk around where possible and observe the Russians as they went about their business. The intelligence officer decided that the best place to gather intelligence was in the marketplaces. He found that traders in the marketplaces were in touch with major Russian garrisons in the area and used the traders to find out about Russian units in the area.[10] He had his people make reports to him in person because of a lack of communications equipment. He was able to gather good information enumerating units and where they were garrisoned, what their needs and consumption were, and what their movements were simply by having people observe what was going on in the course of everyday business.[11]

Another form of HUMINT is called social engineering. Here, inquiries are made, usually by way of impersonation to gather information on how to gain access to sensitive areas or sensitive computer systems. Collectors take advantage of human beings at the controls of the access to either places or things. More specifically, they take advantage of the willingness of those human beings to help, their wish not to be bothered, or their wish not to get in trouble. Such people will do what they can either to help the collector or to get the collector out of their hair by giving the collector sensitive information.[12]

Social engineering also encompasses information that people carelessly throw away, such as phone directories or passwords written on scraps of paper and things like that. A good source for social engineering information comes from Mitnick and Simon's book *The Art of Deception*, in which numerous examples are given of how people have used social engineering to gain access to many sensitive things simply by knowing how to get other human beings to give that information out.

These are all effective means of gathering information. They reside more at the low end of collection compared to what national intelligence agencies engage in. Until now, only OSINT and HUMINT were available to anyone. The degree to which other forms of intelligence could be used was limited mainly by access, and that is the difference today. Technology gives everyone a means to break through that access barrier. Now, all people have access even to technical intelligence when the limits of open source and HUMINT have been reached.

Imagery Intelligence

To understand the advantages of IMINT, we must visualize the historical progression of intelligence gathering that took place to bring it into use. Human beings have always wanted more information on their surroundings. The oldest of our ancestors were limited to what they could see from where they stood. If they wanted to know what lay beyond, they could ask travelers what they had seen. This represents OSINT. They could go to the place about which they were curious themselves or send someone to see it, which may have proved too difficult to do; that would be an example of HUMINT.

At some point, someone probably noticed that it is possible to see more if they could get to a higher elevation. They began climbing trees and high hills, and for millennia that was the only way to get a better look at their surroundings and see what lay beyond where they stood. About 150 years ago, hot air balloons became practical and were used for observation. That breakthrough allowed humanity to ascend to a higher platform and view not only immediate surroundings but also a much larger scope of land than was previously possible, and it could be done from anywhere, assuming that one could bring the balloon anywhere.

Humanity gained the power of flight 100 years ago, and with that we could view not only our surroundings but also any surroundings, often at great distance, up to the range of a plane's fuel tank. Satellites 50 years ago changed the rules of viewing other places. From that time, there were not really any secret or unviewable places. At that point, camouflaging things or keeping them out of view, usually in buildings or underground, became the only way to avoid observation.

Until recently, the higher up one could go, the less access there was for the masses. Only the United States and the Soviet Union had the money and technology to put up satellites. Only they had access to the most professional form of gathering intelligence on surroundings and locations. They used that capability only for military and political considerations of their own. With the passage of time, other satellites were launched; this coincided with the rise of market considerations that rival the military and political considerations of decades past. Many people have wanted or needed satellites for nonmilitary considerations, such as weather and mapping. In a market economy, someone will move to make money from that need. No worldwide governance exists to restrict the use of satellites, so there are only national restrictions on commercial satellites. But, even those restrictions were less a function of governance and more a function of access restriction; that remains true today except the access is now much wider and more available to anyone who wants it.

Why use IMINT? Why does it deliver such advantages? With IMINT, we can see things that are normally inaccessible to us in detail. We can also see a wider area than we could on foot standing on the ground. We can see geographical locations of interest as they are connected to the rest of the world. IMINT offers an outside point of view that is different from looking at something from ground level. At ground level, the horizon may be just across the street, so the access ways to the location are not clear. From higher in the sky, one can see the location of interest and all the roads and rivers that connect to it and obtain much more complete picture of the location.

There are problems that had to be solved to make IMINT practical. One problem was resolution at altitude. That is, fewer small details are readily observable the higher up one goes, particularly if the observation is made only with the human eye. As time progressed, better optics allowed for much more detailed observation of small things, even from space. For instance, in a discussion of satellite photography, discussion of resolution is heard in terms of meters (1-m resolution, 2-m resolution, etc). What this refers to is the smallest object that can be observed at this resolution. So, for instance, at 1-meter resolution objects photographed from space down to the size of 1 m are distinguishable. In fact, resolution exists to be able to read words on mailboxes and maybe smaller. The smaller the resolution, the more detailed the photograph will be and the more information that will be conveyed.

The other problem that IMINT had to overcome is timing. Sophisticated satellites, such as those used by the CIA today, probably have very little time lag from the time that a photograph is taken until it is transmitted to people who analyze and process it. Commercial satellites, on the other hand, probably have a time lag of several hours or more. This is because it is necessary for someone to access the satellite and download the information; the CIA probably has a very sophisticated communications network that allows downloading of information to take place fairly quickly. Commercial satellites at this stage probably do not.

Obviously, information that is most timely is also most useful. However, that is a problem that holds true more for military targets than it does for the type of targets hit in insurgent operations. If the targets are stationary and public, the fact that a photograph might be 12, 24, or 48 hours old may not be as big a concern because obviously a bridge is not going anywhere. Its security may change in a few hours, but that is not the same thing as attempting to discern whether a submarine with nuclear missiles on it is or is not in port.

Right now, private companies answering a market need are supplying IMINT to consumers. There are a number of examples, a few of which are illustrated here. Aerobureau (Great Falls, VA), for instance, takes video footage of inaccessible terrain. This footage is generally sold to news services, showing things like oil spills and damage from natural catastrophes. Aerobureau does this from aircraft that are able to fly over the areas when news camera operators on foot are unable to gain access to these things.[13] There are several companies providing satellite services. Space Imaging (Thornton, CO) advertises a satellite called IKONOS with 1-m resolution capabilities. Their services are diverse and cover business economics, environmental, and security customers.[14] Imagesat International is based in the Netherlands Antilles and Cyprus. Among its customers are governments, and it does in fact do security work, including situation assessments and battle damage assessments.[15] It also assesses infrastructure capabilities, such as transportation, power, and communications.[16] Other companies offer 1-m resolution of cities as well as radar satellites for all weather photography capabilities. Digital Globe (Longmont, CO) offers 1-m or less resolution, which they say is "the highest resolution satellite image commercially available" for mapping, emergency monitoring, and the environment.[17]

The services offered by these companies would probably be expensive to an individual. However, they would probably be quite affordable to an organization or to a government for that matter. These companies sell to anyone with legitimate interests. There do not seem to be any restraints or security mentioned on any of the Web sites for these companies. While it is not being alleged that these companies support insurgencies in any way, it is worth noting that they market capabilities previously owned only by governments.

Judging the effectiveness of this version of satellite intelligence should not be done by old criteria. As we saw in Chapter 3, the targets of the types selected for insurgent operations are not military anymore, but public. The targets are open, public venues or at least unguarded military installations. Although observing the target on foot yields useful information, satellites yield more. With satellites, one can see a wider scope and more complete access to the target. It is also possible to know defenses and surveillance of the area with a wider perspective than one could do on foot. On a more strategic level IMINT allows judgments on target selection. Overall, IMINT offers a less-limited perspective, which allows better judgment to be made on the possibilities for operations. This type of IMINT is probably not on the same level as what the CIA uses, but it can still be quite effective, close enough to plan the types of operations discussed in Chapter 3 on warfare.

Signal Intelligence

Signal intelligence includes intercepting communications.[18] When we talk of intercepting communications, we move from the realm of legality to illegality. There are hints of illegality in other forms of intelligence collection discussed depending on intention, but the active interception of communications unsanctioned by governments is illegal, with or without intention. That is why disclaimers usually come with the sale of surveillance equipment. This is less of a deterrent in war, which generally consists of criminal acts sanctioned by governments.

SIGINT is another type of information to add to the overall intelligence puzzle. In monitoring communications, one finds specific details of timing, intentions, documents, logistics, and conversations. It is possible to obtain this information from HUMINT, but that medium is far more difficult and time consuming than intercepting signal communications. For example, Chechen fighters used to monitor Russian communications to find out what the Russians intended to do operationally during the Chechen wars.[19] Phone conversations, radio talk, pagers, television transmissions, and the Internet are possible avenues for SIGINT collection. The object in collecting information this way is to find out what others are doing or about to do.

How is this done? Which ways are available, and how accessible are they? Listening in on phone conversations can be done either with fiber optics or wireless capabilities. Wireless phone or computer transmissions, for instance, are encrypted, but they are apparently decrypted at the Internet gateway and then reencrypted once transmitted through the gate. This is apparently a window for interception.[20] Cellular scanners can scan for cellular transmissions, which has been against the law since 1994. However, it is apparently possible to modify equipment to engage in this activity.[21] Cell phones and pagers can be tapped or cloned.[22] Digital technology makes it harder but not impossible. Tapping or cloning phones and pagers is partly theft but also partly eavesdropping and intercepting signals depending on location.

Scanners have long been available to monitor police radio traffic. We have already seen that military radio chatter can be monitored if it is not encrypted, and frequencies are not kept secret. That said, it is also not news that criminals, for instance, engaging in criminal activity occasionally will use police scanners to keep apprised of the whereabouts of the police, particularly to know if the police are coming to stop them. This is an example of the use of technology that is open and available on the marketplace for both legal and illegal activity because many people listen to police scanners purely out of interest.

The Internet is probably the most lucrative place to gather information. It not only contains information but also encompasses making wealth and communicating ideas. There are multiple vulnerabilities to the Internet because of the necessary openness of the system. This cross connects with social engineering problems discussed in this chapter; people attempt to gain the means to access sensitive information even when it is protected on the Internet. Even the Defense Department is not immune to break-ins, mainly of its unclassified sites.[23] Once inside, people look for information stored on a system to download; usually, this information is not protected.

The interesting thing about this sort of SIGINT done on the Internet is that in many cases it is not done by professional intelligence services. Indeed, much of what is done, colloquially known as *hacking*, is done by private citizens who have pioneered many of the techniques in use. Indeed, there is a journal, *2600: The Hacker Quarterly*, that catalogs the vulnerabilities of software, phone systems, and the Internet. No judgment is passed here on cataloging such vulnerabilities. However, it is worth noting that the people cataloging these vulnerabilities are not working for government intelligence agencies.

Instead, they bring their own unique (in some cases "home-grown") knowledge of the vulnerabilities.

Collection of information has probably never been more open to the private citizen as it is right now, but collection is only part of the equation. Collected information must be made legible and useful, which leads to a discussion of analysis and production of the collected information.

Analysis and Production

Once data is collected, it must be converted to something that can inform decision making. This could be done by way of making a written report. It could be done through the processing and enhancement of photographs. It could be done by developing timelines of events or behavior. It could be done by any combination of the above. Generally, information is condensed into a medium that is most useful to the consumers who want the information. Anyone engaged in any type of decision making on any subject collects information and makes it useful for their decision making.

In the post–cold war era, businesses have seen the value in this and created the first modern nongovernmental intelligence capabilities. These capabilities have taken the form of political risk analysis and competitive intelligence. Political risk analysis assesses the political risk of foreign ventures. Competitive intelligence tracks future trends and possibilities in business. These things are not industrial espionage so much as they are open source analysis.

Analysis and production form the critical link between collection and decision making. Correct and relevant interpretation of information presented in readily digestible form is necessary for successful decision making. Presentation must be made in a useful and understandable way. Different decision makers also need different products. The trick is to find out what decision makers need and in what form to make their decisions. If the information is not presented in a useful form, then the information is not useful; in many cases, that means it will not be used or perceived to be useful. This will lead to either bad decision making or decision making without intelligence, either of which can be catastrophic.

The problem is that all information can be variably interpreted. The term *connect the dots* should be read accurately. In the child's game of that name, sequence is key; connecting dots in the right way yields the right picture. Connecting dots in the wrong way yields little of use even with the right information. As an example, recall the attack on Pearl Harbor, for which in retrospect there seemed to be a good deal of warning that the Japanese were going to make the attack on the United States. The same can be said for the attack on the World Trade Center and the Pentagon on September 11.

The point is that now more people are playing the intelligence game. Not all are bound by conventional wisdom that tends to permeate structured conventional intelligence agencies. The new players produce estimates that are serviceable and effective to their own decision makers. That said, all such products are still controlled and confronted by the eternal intelligence problem: Decision makers draw their own conclusions when the intelligence product is disseminated to them.

Dissemination

Dissemination is about getting the relevant information into the hands of the right decision makers. The decision makers can request the information that they want, which is the easy way to do things. But, producers must also know when the information they collected is relevant to a decision maker and direct that information to the relevant person. Dissemination is now about the Internet and its myriad abilities to transfer information. This really is what allows amateur intelligence to be truly global. Imagine trying to send volumes of reports, photos, or maps by mail or phone. It would be too impractical. Giving information over the phone cannot communicate graphics. Mail takes time to move from one place to another.

These problems hint at tests of successful dissemination. Dissemination must be as complete as possible. It must also be timely. Without both of these components, dissemination fails. Completeness is subject to timeliness, and timeliness is the caveat on completeness. What this means is that it is necessary to develop as complete a picture as possible in a timely fashion. If one waits until the picture is absolutely complete, the time when it is useful may have passed. On the other hand, it may not be possible to gather complete information before the time that it is needed. It is often necessary to deliver the warning that the picture is not complete because there was not enough time to gather all the possible information.

The Internet is the key to passing the dissemination tests. It delivers information in great volume very quickly and cheaply. Its capabilities expand to meet market needs and new ideas. It is faster, in some cases, than the government-designed systems although not as well protected in all cases. The open Internet is not as well guarded as government intelligence systems, which means it is possible for the open Internet to be corrupted and its information to be intercepted by one's opponents. However, for mercurial organizations, a mercurial Internet may work better than a formal infrastructure, which could be found and destroyed. In this case, movement probably substitutes for security. The fact that distance is not a factor in transmission allows movements to be global, much like Al Qaeda. But, dissemination must not be wrapped up in technology. The Internet is a great tool, but the tool only works when it is managed well. Information technology facilitates things. Because human beings make and receive information, they must be efficient for intelligence to work.

Intelligence is used for planning and decision making, but intelligence can also be used to mobilize the masses, plead cases, and recruit support. This intelligence utilizes another type of dissemination. For this type of dissemination, one might use Web sites, radio, or television. The object is to speak to the world and deliver whatever message is the political objective of the organization. The bottom line is that dissemination is the key to making information affect action. The type of action, the decision makers, and the objective come together to decide the practical execution. Popular access makes nongovernmental intelligence practical; the Internet makes it global.

Sabotage

It is worth discussing sabotage as a function of intelligence. The term sabotage is used here with a caveat. In a certain context, all the warfare described in this book could be considered sabotage. We want to distinguish between physical and nonphysical destruction. With that in mind, sabotage here is about using information as a weapon to target other information. The point is to show that sabotage can be effective; indeed, it has been effective, and amateurs have been doing it. This is not going to be a "how-to" handbook on information sabotage or another cautionary treatise on the evils of hacking. It is enough simply to scan the possibilities.

The scope of these actions varies because of invasiveness. The actions could be as small as defacing Web sites, as has been done to numerous Web sites, including those at the National Aeronautic and Space Administration, the CIA, and the Department of Justice.[24] On the other hand, the actions could be as large scale as counterfeiting. There are reports of counterfeiting credit cards, which could be quite dangerous to all other forms of information brokerage because the act encompasses both economic damage and identity theft.[25] There are other reports of Syria and Iran counterfeiting U.S. dollars to pay debts and finance operations that could be injurious to the American economy.[26] Counterfeiting can also include other documents, such as fake passports and drivers' licenses.

Hacking can be used not only to steal information but also to create power outages that cause downtime to computers and other forms of machinery, resulting in lost productivity and lost money. Here are some examples. The Tamil Tigers, in their war with the Sri Lankan Government, flooded e-mail servers at Sri Lankan embassies around the world, rendering them incapable for a time of receiving e-mail.[27] Hackers have disabled phone company computers, resulting in cutting off Worcester Airport in Massachusetts for 6 hours.[28] Reports alleged that some utilities receive more than 1 million cyber intrusions per year.[29] Power outages have caused billions of dollars of lost revenue to companies that rely on data storage to do their business.[30]

False information is also a weapon used to affect intelligence and lead decision makers to false conclusions. If the false information is successful, those decision makers make bad decisions that have adverse effects on the actions that are subsequently taken. The Chechens, for instance, used to give false orders on clear radio transmissions to mislead Russian soldiers regarding their positions and intentions.[31] This sort of deception leads people to either make the wrong moves (if they do not know they are being deceived) or question those moves and go slower until they are sure what is happening (if they think they are being deceived).

Some methods use science literally to destroy information. A man named David Schreiner, for instance, attempted to demonstrate what he called high-energy radio frequency (HERF) guns. The purpose of these guns is to focus an electromagnetic pulse on electronics, which can crash computers and disable cars. It is claimed that this can be done at distances of up to 100 feet. During Info War Con 99, this was demonstrated.[32] It is not clear whether the results are predictable or that such a gun would be useful in all circumstances, but the possibility of it cannot be ignored. It presents the possibility of the mobile destruction of electronics anywhere at any time. Any building reachable by car could be targeted. The possibility of this suggests that it would be necessary for electrical equipment, particularly sensitive electrical equipment, to be protected from electromagnetic pulse; this could be both expensive and time consuming.

In an information-driven world, information can be an effective weapon in the right context. It can deny the use of necessary tools and attending information. It can be used to delay or confuse other decision makers. That said, it is not an effective substitute for violence. Information denial can be fixed. There will often be a delay, and this is bad. But, destruction calls for replacement or going without, and that is worse. The proof of relative effectiveness is in usage and success. Physical acts cause tangible damage; information acts do not (yet), although the potential is there. Plus, information attacks have not yielded logistical physical costs on a scale that would disrupt a military operation, but it is probably only a matter of time until that happens.

Organized Crime

Organized crime presents an element to the intelligence issue that is unclear but potentially dangerous. Criminal organizations have intelligence capabilities necessary to their own operations, and these could be used by other organizations. For instance, some Russian criminal organizations have people with intelligence training who provide the organization with warnings of police operations or those of rival organizations.[33] Reports exist that former Soviet KGB (State Security Commission) officers have joined Russian organized crime.[34] In Colombia, the Cali drug cartel developed intelligence on its main rival, the Medellin cartel.[35]

Indeed, governments have used organized crime for intelligence work in the past. As an example, in World War II the Office of Naval Intelligence utilized organized crime figure Lucky Luciano and his influence on the New York City waterfront for counterintelligence purposes against Nazi agents working in New York.[36]

So, the possibility of criminal organizations taking part in intelligence operations exists. If it is a reality, the possibilities for private intelligence expand greatly. If this chapter shows nothing else, it is that a market exists beyond governments for intelligence, and people will move to meet the needs of the market. If those in organized crime have capabilities for this market and sense that there is money to be made, they will move to meet those needs eventually. If they do not have the capabilities, they may go and get them, as they have done for other market needs.

The implications of issue organizations having the ability to hire intelligence capabilities are serious. It means that they might be able to buy professional-level intelligence capabilities. If we believe that former Russian intelligence agents are working for Russian organized crime currently, if information is for sale now to anyone who cares to buy it, then there is a much more pronounced need on the part of governments (or anyone else) for counterintelligence. This means not only the need for better information protection but also greater costs.

Intelligence is a necessary part of all warfare. It is no longer the province of governments alone. Many others can also practice the collection and dissemination of intelligence. Private concerns, amateur sleuths, organizations, and businesses all want it and can get it. It is facilitated by technology but not driven by it. The keys to success are the same as for warfare in general. The needs of the political agenda drive actions. The actions require information to be successful. Now, that information is available to anyone, making the success of their operations more possible than ever before.

Chapter 5

FUNDING, PROCUREMENT, AND TRAINING

Books are written and movies are made about the actions of war, but none of that action is possible without support in the form of funding, training, and procurement. Issue constellations and other forms of insurgency must support their efforts just as national armed forces must. But, although national armed forces are able in some part to do it in the open (not that they always do), insurgencies by their nature cannot. This means they need to find ways to fund, train, and arm their forces outside of legal means and in a way that is less visible to or trackable by their opponents. In the past, this has led insurgencies to make clandestine deals with patron governments. Increasingly, nongovernmental means, such as private brokers and organized crime, have come to the forefront of a growing market.

Organized crime stands as a good example of the possibility of supporting war by nongovernmental means. It should surprise no one, then, that criminal organizations play a part in war and have throughout history. They may be facilitators, moving arms around and giving intelligence between governments that do not officially connect to each other. They can provide conduits for the sale of goods in illicit markets. Sometimes, they have capabilities or access to things that people and even governments need but for whatever reason do not have.

In Russia, various organized crime factions play a large part in the Russian economy and allegedly do business with the Russian military. The Russian and Chechen mob help distribute goods and services (automobiles, personal security) without the red tape associated with the government.[1] This comes at a cost to the economy because often the mobsters pocket a substantial profit, but it is tolerated because they also facilitate the economy in the region. The sale of drugs and weapons brought the Chechen mob 10–15 million rubles per week.[2] This trade often was carried out in view of a substantially dismantled internal security apparatus.

The role these mobsters play in facilitating war is that of weapons dealer. It is a lucrative business, particularly when supplied by an army starved for cash. Soldiers in the Russian military allegedly used the mob to sell weapons (including uranium) to Third World countries.[3] This includes reports of mule trains bringing uranium to Afghanistan.[4] The mob is also responsible for transporting military materials such as titanium and aluminum (a raid captured 340 railcars filled with these elements).[5]

World War II saw the participation of criminal organizations in both the Atlantic and Pacific theaters of war. In a total war for total victory, ultimately anything useful will be brought to bear. As the war started, a battle for control of the Atlantic Ocean began. German submarines were sinking massive tonnages of Allied shipping just off the American coast. With good reason, the U.S. Navy was concerned about sabotage and espionage by German spies along the New York waterfront and launched Operation Underworld.[6] They used Lucky Luciano, who even from prison ran the New York waterfront, to uncover Nazi spies as well as facilitate the invasion of Sicily.[7] Luciano's assistance was effective, and soon the U.S. Navy began shutting down spy organizations assisting the German U-boats. Luciano was released from prison after the war and deported to Italy. This is an instance for which the partnership between government and mobster was quietly effective; not all such partnerships were.

In China at the same time, the triads (Chinese organized crime) had a role in the conduct of Nationalist China's wars against Japan and the Communists. The triads had infiltrated the ruling Kuomintang nationalist party. Reports persist that before becoming head of the Nationalists, Chiang was involved in robbery, extortion, and assassination. Triad men were installed in key government positions. Soon, the triads had a brigade in the Nationalist Army, and one of their members was made governor of Shanghai.[8]

The triads supplied weapons and security to the Nationalists. They could procure weaponry that the Nationalists had trouble convincing Western nations to sell them. The triads were used to put down Communist uprisings, something they did in a particularly bloody fashion. They were paid millions of dollars by the Shanghai merchants for that purpose. The triads became the secret police in return for a free hand in Shanghai. This allowed Chiang to engage in criminal activity while looking clean to the governments of the world.[9]

In the war, the triads assisted downed fliers and provided intelligence to the Allies on Japanese activities. However, they did not let the war get in the way of making money. They also ran gambling and prostitution in the Japanese occupied areas. This it seems was done less to gain valuable intelligence and more to keep a flow of money coming in from both sides of the war.[10]

Criminal organizations seemed actually not to fight in wars. Instead, the part they played in these examples was facilitation of the combatants, always with an eye to the opportunity to make some money from the affair. It is worth listing the services they can provide to combatants, both government and non-state organizations. The mob apparently can facilitate government arms sales, provide intelligence, provide security, and do these tasks without implicating governments. This usually comes at a cost that can be economically debilitating and embarrassing, leading to crackdowns by other arms of government with the passage of time.

Globalism means that this facilitation can now be made worldwide. The Russian mob sells Russian arms in many places worldwide, as does the Chechen mob. The Ukrainian mob traffics in weaponry, possibly weapons of mass destruction (WMD).[11] There is a market for weapons that must pass under the notice of the more powerful nations of the world. Still, the mob has proved useful as a back channel to governments because the rules of the world political scene no longer preclude access. It is important to recognize that organized crime can work with issue constellations to the same effect. Any investigation of issue constellations will probably be brought to investigate whether or if transnational organized crime is involved.

There is a famous saying among military planners that "amateurs talk strategy, but professionals talk logistics." That statement is very important to the conduct of warfare. One cannot just go to war. Fielding an army requires support. What makes the Normandy invasion unique, for instance, is how hard it was (and still is) to supply thousands of ships and millions of people for an operation. Support is complex. It covers food, water, gas, ammunition, training, building/repair, and the money to pay for it all. Much of the American defense budget covers these things, which is the reason why American power projection capabilities have been so successful over the years. It is also why America alone does it on a regular basis and has no equals in the performance of it. Although America is the best at supporting war, it is possible for others to be effective, if not spectacular.

A full discussion of warfare support is beyond the scope of this book. Instead, this discussion is more general, focusing on three basic areas: funding, procurement, and training. These functions are less complex for insurgencies than for conventional armed forces, and they are smaller in scope. Funding covers ways in which insurgencies gather, store, and exchange money. Procurement talks about the type of weapons bought, from who, and how. Training covers information, education, and practice, as well as the degree to which those things are accessible to the average person today. Overall, this chapter surveys the simplicity and effectiveness of the systems commonly in place or constructed for supporting insurgencies and the degree to which they feed into insurgency warfare and the political goals attending them.

Funding

There is a broad spectrum of funding possibilities for insurgencies. There is legitimate funding, that is, gathering funding within the laws of the land where that gathering takes place. There is illegitimate funding, or gathering funding outside the laws of the particular country. There is a third alternative, which can be called tainted finding. This is funding from legitimate fronts that appear legitimate to the unknowing but that nevertheless gather money to support the insurgency.

Legally, one could construct a funding system from any combination of the above. The funding can come from any group. Largely, this is a function of where the funding is being gathered, where funding is needed, and which opportunities are available in a given location. If it is possible to make money through legitimate means, one could do that. Starting a legitimate business has the virtue of not calling attention to the insurgency in a particular area. If it is impossible to start a business or if money is needed faster than it would take by starting a business that makes money, crime is also a possible fundraiser. One could find benefactors willing to donate money to the cause or just solicit donations broadly, hoping for a quantity of donations that would equate to a large amount of money.

Gray areas develop when one can distinguish between knowing and unknowing contributors. Some people donate directly to insurgency, and the donation gives them a direct tie to the insurgency. Such people probably do not care that they are being tied to the insurgency. One could also build a charity with a charitable purpose, in which case the contributors do not necessarily know the background of the charity. HAMAS (the Islamic Resistance Movement), for instance, has been known to gather funds through charities and NGOs.[12] The Benevolence International Foundation was shut down for funding Al Qaeda.[13] Central Intelligence Agency reports have stated that as many as 33% of Islamic NGOs give some kind of support to known insurgent organizations.[14]

Fundraising is not limited to funds from just the willing. It is also possible to gather funds from the unwilling and the unwary. Many people want to give money to help the underprivileged around the world. Very few contributors probably perform the background checks regarding where that money ultimately goes.

There are many possible sources of money available to insurgencies, from just a short list consisting of legitimate businesses, benefactors, the unwitting, and criminal organizations. Some insurgencies could use all of the above. Others may only use legitimate businesses. The degree to which any of them wants to operate outside the system is probably the degree to which they will include more legitimate or illegitimate ways of gathering money.

There is an interesting aspect to be considered in talking about funding. Funding is not just about legitimate and illegitimate means of gathering money. There is also a question of permanent, semipermanent, and nonpermanent means of gathering funding. Not all funding structures are permanent, particularly in the Eastern Hemisphere. How does one judge the permanence of a funding system? One way is by looking at the infrastructure and formality of the system, that is, the degree to which records are kept, standard operating procedures are observed, and there are physical structures involved for the gathering and transfer of funds; all help decide the permanence of the system.

This permanence delivers a reliability and lack of risk that the world's financiers like and drives them to participate in this system more than other systems. The banks that service the legitimate world are part of that formal system, as are the buildings that assist in the banking system. The permanent system also includes phone lines and planes, ships, trains, and cars used to transfer funds, goods, and services back and forth across countries, across continents, and around the world. It also consists of the records that are kept of these various transfers, as well as lending and credit. The formal system has well-established processes for gathering, storing, and transmitting funds as well as using them. There are also well-established procedures for recording and tracking those transactions. This is meant to build faith among users, who power the system and give it this permanence.

An insurgency could build such a system and have its own permanent funding system or use the existing one. Although a permanent system has a well-established record for success, that system can be tracked and co-opted or destroyed like any other physical, permanent system. The insurgency would then be at the mercy of any enemy with a stronger economy. However, there are other alternatives that also serve insurgent funding.

Insurgencies could use a system that already exists, such as the permanent banking system, but they would use it on a semipermanent basis. What this means is that the insurgency can evacuate the system if it feels that it has been tracked or in danger. The system is used but not owned by the insurgency, so there is less worry about funding problems if the system gets destroyed. It is after all, the permanent system that everyone uses so probably it will not be destroyed. The difficulty of using a semipermanent system, particularly one that already exists and is used by the legitimate world, is that it is easier to track by the system's own watchdogs. That said, it is always possible to abandon the system at any sign of trouble, and it allows (temporarily at least) for volumes of money to be moved as long as no one is counting on utilizing the accounts that are established over the long term.

It is also possible to avoid the established world financial system. This is the nonpermanent path. It does not utilize physical infrastructure, and the formality and permanence described here does not exist with this type of system. Indeed, the system exists when it is needed but requires less maintenance. Its very lack of formal physical infrastructure makes it very difficult to track or destroy. It is probably the least trackable system, as discussed in this section. Sometimes, no records are kept in this system, which makes it very difficult even to know if some sort of illicit transfer of funds is ongoing. This system is just as effective if not as large or as efficient as the permanent world banking system.

Legitimate and illegitimate funding feed into permanent, semipermanent, and nonpermanent systems. Obviously, the more insurgent funds are kept hidden, the better for them. We can explore funding in terms of hiding funds gathered by various means in various types of system. This hints at breaking this exploration of funding into three parts—currency, fundraising, and transfer—and how these parts are obtained and used. The formal banking system is known very well and is useful as a baseline for describing alternatives. This is the system that people use every day in one form or another to get paychecks, save money, pay bills, invest, and get loans.

The word *currency* implies money to most people. That money comes in the form of paper, coin, or a check. But, the reality is that there are three types of currency that can be used. We forget that we once were a world that used gold and jewels as currency, and our exchange of goods and services was expressed in terms of precious metal and precious stones. On the other end of the spectrum, however, we now use electronic money, that is, money that only exists electronically and is not physical in the developed world. We use this on a regular basis in the form of credit cards, debit cards, and so forth. The current world banking system uses paper and electronic money.

Whether our preference is paper or plastic, money is faster and easier to use to buy things than other currency. It is also faster and easier to track. This is because paper and electronic money come with trackable serial numbers and well-kept records. Gold and jewels, on the other hand, are less trackable. Which currency a given cell or group might use is probably a function of need, and security may dictate that gold and jewels are the currency to be used.

On the other hand, expediency may dictate that paper or electronic money would be the best medium. Again, using the system exposes the insurgency to system watchdogs. Governments have resources and experience in tracking illegal activity. Governments also cooperate with each other to track interaction across countries and around the world. For insurgencies, this fact makes going covert and working outside the system even more necessary for survival. Although credit is probably the most trackable form of currency, it is still used. It has been documented that insurgents around the world still use credit and debit cards.[15]

It is possible to do all of the above (i.e., use currency consisting of gold and jewels, money and coin, credit, and debit cards), keeping large sums of money out of the system and utilizing small sums of money within the permanent system. This way, the overall finances of the insurgency are protected by secrecy, but it is still possible to fund the cells that serve the insurgency.

Al Qaeda seems to have converted some of its funds to gold and diamonds, perhaps as early as 1998, selling the gems at a later date for cash and making it difficult to track.[16] Lebanese Hizbollah similarly funded themselves with African diamonds.[17] Although the phenomenon has existed apparently for quite some time, it was not until after September 11 that it was brought to the attention of the world.[18] This almost certainly is because American efforts to freeze Al Qaeda funds forced those insurgents to convert their funds into other currency, and the volume of that conversion became noticeable. But, the form of currency is only the start of the discussion.

Over time, funds begin to accumulate and must be stored somehow. The sums are not small. The U.S. government estimated that HAMAS has an annual budget of $50 million.[19] In 2000, the Holy

Land Foundation for Relief and Development (a designated terrorist organization supporter) raised $13 million.[20] Al Qaeda diamond smugglers have been caught with information detailing $20 to $50 million in funds to buy surface-to-air missiles (SAMs).[21] Overall, it is estimated that $200 million pass through Islamic charities each year, and apparently some of it is diverted knowingly or unknowingly to insurgents.[22] This is not a phenomenon relegated to the Middle East. The United Self Defense Forces of Colombia (AUC) in Colombia has attempted to buy arms with $25 million in drug profits.[23]

As stated, the funds can come from legal or illegal sources, from those who give knowingly and those who give unwittingly. Donations can be used either by individual benefactors or through charities. For instance, the Palestinian Children's Relief Fund has been linked to the Holy Land Foundation for Relief and Development.[24] Al Qaeda also uses charities for funding, even chanelling the money to support other organizations like the Moro National Liberation Front and Abu Sayyaf in the Philippines.[25] Another organization, the SAAR Foundation, showed a tax return that gave $9 million to charity. The actual donation money seems to have disappeared. Investigators allege it went to support terrorism.[26] These are just a few examples of large sums of money raised for insurgency using charitable foundations as a front.

Starting a business can be profitable whether illegal or illegal. On the illegal side, it has been noted that insurgencies in the past have used drugs, credit card fraud, illegally sold cigarettes, stolen infant formula, and the sale of knockoff clothing to fund their operations.[27] Criminal operations are not bounded just by fraud. According to the Federal Bureau of Investigation, much more vicious crimes have been perpetrated in support of insurgency. These crimes include extortion, kidnapping, arms trafficking, and cyber crime.[28] Again, the sums can be quite large. The Kurdish Worker's Party (PKK) is said to make $40 million a year from drug trafficking.[29] At the same time, insurgencies have started legitimate businesses, such as those dealing with auto or home repair, to fund their operations.[30]

Starting a business of any kind is a solid way to fund insurgency in the long term. It is profitable and unregulated, particularly the criminal aspects, and that works well for insurgency. Here when we say unregulated, we mean criminal enterprises that by their nature are done without the knowledge of government. There are few records and no taxation involved, which means the money is all profit, and it is off the radar of government trackers until something calls their attention to it.

Gathering money is useful only if it can be stored safely and transferred quickly. It is possible to store the money in banks, but money in banks can be tracked; if it can be tracked, it can be impounded, in which case the funds are lost. This is not to say that it is never tried. The Muslim Brotherhood started their own bank in the Bahamas for a time to serve both Al Qaeda and HAMAS.[31]

Another way to store the money would be to convert it to gold and diamonds and stash it someplace until it is needed. The problem is that gold and diamonds cannot be used operationally very easily. So, operational sums seem to use the established banking system in the form of checks, Western Union transfers, debit cards, or paper money.[32] Perhaps assimilation is the key to figuring out how the money is stored until needed. In other words, in a given operational area, whatever people are using for money in that area is probably the conversion type for the funds. As large sums, they could be stored, at least in the most popular instances, as gold and jewels.

Finding a money transfer system that exists off the radar of the permanent system watchdogs is not as difficult as people might think. Indeed, such a system has existed since before the formal banking system the world currently uses. It is called *hawala*.

The hawala is a way of transferring goods or money without using physical currency or goods. Instead, the transfer takes place among networks of brokers (called hawaladars).[33] But, unlike Western fund transfers based on scrupulous record keeping, hawaladars base their transfers on trust that other hawaladars will honor their end of the transfer without such records. For example, someone could give money to a hawaladar in America to send to a relative in the Middle East. That hawaladar will contact a counterpart in the Middle East and tell the counterpart to give money to the relative in that area. The two hawaladars will then settle the debt among themselves at a later date by exchanging goods, services, or cash worth the amount sent to the relative. It can all be done quickly with a phone call. No record will exist of who sent the money or to whom it was sent. This is a perfect setup for insurgent funding.[34]

The hawaladars might be regular business partners and could bury the financial transfer among their normal business transactions. In the example, the debt might be covered by the American hawaladar sending extra goods to the Middle Eastern partner totaling the amount given to the relative. Still no record would exist of the original transaction between the person in America who first approached the hawaladar and the person's relative in the Middle East.[35]

This system is both efficient and reliable. It is estimated that remittance takes 2 days at most. It also has fewer points to pass through between principals, which makes for a smoother tranmission. Hawaladars do not keep records of these transactions, and that technically makes this system a form of tax evasion in many countries. But, it also allows transactions to take place outside the system, which is appealing to many people helping to perpetuate the system.[36] It is based on trust (that is what hawala means) that all brokers are going to carry out the transaction. The fact that it has existed for so long is a testament to the fact that brokers observe the obligation diligently, and this makes the system reliable as well as untraceable.[37]

The amount of money moving through hawala is quite large. Pakistani officials estimate that $2 million to $3 million a day is delivered from Pakistan to Dubai.[38] The economies of India, Pakistan, Afghanistan, and many other nations use hawala. In many cases, they have nationals working in other nations who send the money they make back home, where it is put into local economies. As a result, there is little incentive to stop hawala. In 1998, India's hawala had over $600 billion moving through it.[39]

Obviously, on the face of it the hawala system is not permanent or official in the sense of a formal banking system. It appears to be a value exchange system between two or more brokers. In other words, two or more brokers exchange value (which could be goods, services, money, or even favors) with each other totaling the amount of money transferred from one broker to another. They settle among themselves, who owes what to whom. Because very little record keeping is done, much can be disguised as money is transferred back and forth. This allows for moving not only cash, but also goods, services, and commodities (like gold and jewels). It is not as efficient as Western banking systems (or it would be used by the world instead), but it is less trackable and more flexible than those systems. It has what can best be described as a floating infrastructure. That is, the infrastructure is more about the connection between people that it is the formal, physical infrastructure that Westerners envision, with buildings and phone lines and things like that.

There are many ways for the brokers to be in touch with each other, with one much like another. The key is the connection, the relationship between the brokers, wherever those brokers may be. As long as that connection exists, this floating infrastructure also exists. A floating infrastructure allows the connection for both legal and illegal funding. It can allow for the funding of legal things such as travel and illegal things such as the purchase of weapons. It has limits. A hawala system probably cannot fund and outfit an army to national government army standards, especially the government of the United States, but Hawala is perfect for funding insurgency.

The overall picture uses combinations of currency gathered both legally and illegally, stores it in a variety of places, and utilizes combinations of finance systems that are permanent, semipermanent, and nonpermanent. It is possible for insurgencies to gather large sums of money with less chance of discovery or undue attention and to disperse those sums of money, both to hide from the eyes of governments and to put into the hands of operational insurgents to fund their operations. This is the measure of effectiveness for insurgent funding, and it is possible for anyone to utilize it.

Procurement

Procurement is available to anyone. Anything can be bought or gotten somehow. Much that could not be bought can also either be made or stolen. Location has an influence on the legality, the markets, the brokers in those markets, and in some ways the entire system. Assuming there is money, legal things like communications equipment can always be bought. Dreams of bloodless warfare aside, the insurgencies of the future will fight, and they will require weapons to fight their wars.

Buying weapons has become easier since the fall of communism. There are fewer restrictions or strings attached to buying weapons. In many places around the world, there are plentiful arsenals in the hands of cash-poor countries waiting to be bought by anyone who has the money in spite of international agreements or national regulations. Procurement becomes easier still if the weapons involved are not large or technologically sophisticated. That is, small arms and light crewed weaponry have become much easier to acquire by anyone who wants them than they ever have been. Weapons that are low tech, less expensive, easily transported, and less noticeable have caught the eye of a much larger market that has developed since the fall of communism.

In the past, insurgencies relied on a national patron or captured weapons to arm themselves to fight wars. This is how the idea of state-sponsored terrorism came to be. Again, because terrorism largely is a question of whether a given group's violence is considered legitimate or illegitimate, a given nation sponsoring an insurgency group would receive that name if the insurgents' group was considered a terrorist organization. Giving the insurgency weapons and in some cases funding would then make that nation a state sponsor of terrorist organizations.

It is possible to buy these weapons, at least some of them, legally in some countries, but there is an access problem in that, even in countries where some of these weapons are legal, the degree to which laws and conventions are enforced may mean that the weapons cannot be bought openly and cannot be bought without what is called an end-user certificate stating where the arms will be sent and for what purpose.[40] However, in other places, regulations are lax and not enforced diligently. In places like this, it is easier to get weapons if there is money available. Insurgencies do not always have state sponsors. This is particularly true in the post-Communist, post-September 11 world, in which an economic giant like the United States and its allies, who also are quite strong economically, are watching and waiting for insurgencies to show themselves as having a state sponsor. Governments can punish each other quite harshly for engaging in state sponsorship of "terrorism." Many countries will either swear off that sponsorship or will find a way to disguise it. In any case, at least currently, it is unlikely that any government will allow itself to be linked to terrorism in any way knowing the wrath that awaits it.

Because state sponsorship has become impractical in the current context, insurgencies look to brokers or organized crime to obtain weapons. Organized crime has been trafficking in weapons for centuries. They have a long history of doing this and making money at it. Mobsters have been caught trafficking weapons to the Red Brigades in Italy.[41] To facilitate their weapons trafficking, they have placed corrupt officials in the only Russian government agency to authorize weapons exports.[42] There were even reports of Russian mobsters attempting to buy the whole Hungarian arms industry before they were stopped.[43]

Other weapons can be made instead of bought if the knowledge exists but the money does not. For instance, the Oklahoma City, Oklahoma, bombers made their bomb out of diesel fuel and fertilizer, two commonly available compounds that, when combined, made a powerful explosive. The bomb that was used in Oklahoma City was powerful enough to destroy half of the 16-story concrete Murrah Federal Building. Making explosives with commonly available substances is another way that insurgencies can procure weapons and keep "under the radar" of the governments that are looking for them. This is because the items that they are buying are not explicit. They are everyday components that can be used for a number of things. Farmers buy diesel fuel and fertilizer. Insurgents can easily hide the motives of their purchases among similar compounds bought by farmers. Also, this makes it very hard for government investigators to distinguish between insurgents and law-abiding citizens.

To understand weapons procurement better, we can divide weapons into small-, medium-, and large-size arms, and criteria for each of these categories are as follows. Small-size arms are individual weaponry. They are cheap. They are easy transportable and can be gotten in large numbers fairly easily. Midsize arms are things usable by a single or small group of insurgents for tactical operations. Midsize arms include artillery and heavy machine guns and require a certain level of training and understanding beyond what low-level armaments utilize. Finally, large-size arms are complex machines of fairly large size and expense requiring a good deal of training and carrying a good deal of destructive power (e.g., tanks and aircraft).

With these definitions in mind, it is possible to enumerate low-end weapons as including pistols and rifles, small explosives, and rocket-propelled grenades. Midlevel weaponry would be manned portable air defense rockets (MANPADs) and other forms of crew-served weaponry. High-level weapons would include tanks, ships, and WMD.

Most weapons are available these days if there is a market and money ready to be spent to obtain them. If there is an identified need, someone will move to fill the need, and nothing should be ruled out. Indeed, there is a tale of a Russian mobster brokering the sale of a Russian Foxtrot submarine (that is, regular navy diesel submarine) to the drug dealer Pablo Escobar to smuggle drugs to various parts of the world; the sale (which was stopped by authorities) was complete with a captain and crew of 17 for $100 million.[44]

Insurgencies seem to favor small-size weapons. They are more easily stored and hidden. They are more easily transported. They can be bought in larger quantities and are cheaper. Training is easier and less expensive. There are a larger number of sellers and brokers.[45] Lax enforcement of regulations contributes to this ease of procurement, particularly in the developing world.[46]

WMD are a concern all over the world today. The new openness of markets to various types of weaponry and the availability of the knowledge to make them mean that WMD used by insurgents are a possibility today in a way that would not have been conceived before 20 years ago. That said, making and using WMD effectively are not simple matters with predictable results. Aum Shinrikyo's attempts to use nerve gas in the Tokyo subway system illustrate that fact. The nerve gas they made and attempted to use in the Tokyo subway system had some effect. People did die from it, but it was nowhere near the catastrophe they envisioned because the use of these weapons and their results are not a foregone conclusion the way bullets and explosives are.

WMD are usable if the knowledge exists to make them. But, even with that knowledge an insurgent group still needs specific materials to make those weapons. Those materials are still hard to get, although not as hard as they once were. It also must be said that for such weapons to be useful in any way, the weapons must produce very specific reactions under very specific conditions, and that is harder still. Nevertheless, the knowledge is widely available (a subject discussed in more detail in this section). Suffice it to say that building and execution are more possible than they were but are not easy.

What has changed is that now materials are available even to make the attempt. Chemicals are available commercially. Biological materials are also available commercially to a point. Nuclear materials are not available commercially, but they can be made available once again, depending on money and market and finding the right broker. Reports persist of uranium trafficking. The mob has allegedly been a pipeline to sell uranium to developing nations.[47] There are also tales of mob couriers moving uranium from Uzbekistan into Afghanistan.[48] In 2002, smugglers were tried in Minsk for trafficking in nuclear fuel rods.[49] There are many more stories of nuclear, biological, and chemical materials changing hands in various ways and with varying degrees of accuracy. These examples serve to illustrate the change of conditions since the cold war that make insurgent use of WMD a possibility.

Still, there are good reasons why armies do not use WMD as a matter of course. The results of these weapons are not predictable. It is possible to kill friendly forces with them and contaminate areas that must subsequently be occupied by friendly forces. Insurgency groups do not always care about that last reason, or even the one before it, but the first probably is always a consideration for them. This is because insurgencies generally do not have a wealth of weapons of any kind to spend to no purpose or to obtain no results. It would be bad for them to utilize such weapons and not get the catastrophic results that they desired in using WMD.

That was America's dilemma when developing the first atomic bomb. It was feared that the bomb itself might never work, so dropping it without knowing if it worked would be counterproductive to the war effort and a waste of $1 billion. That is why the bomb was tested in the New Mexico desert to be sure that it worked. It is a problem for insurgents. An insurgent can develop the weapons, but without tests the insurgents can never know for sure if a weapon works to the desired degree. Governments can practice these things. Governments can gather this information, but insurgents cannot without being caught and attacked, and that is one of the main difficulties of using WMD that are homemade. This is why buying them already made will probably be better than building them for insurgents. Buying them is hard but not impossible.

It is difficult to obtain definite numbers on weapon transfers because many weapons transfers are done illegally. For example, in the

Ukraine it is estimated that only 20% of total arms exports were officially sanctioned by the government in 1996. Italian law enforcement estimated traffickers smuggled 13,000 tons of weapons from the Ukraine, including rifles, missiles, and antitank weapons.[50] Shipments to Africa have been known to be quite large. One such shipment totaled up to 68 tons of weapons delivered in 1999 to the Revolutionary United Front (RUF) in Sierra Leone.[51]

Obviously, large numbers of small arms and light weapons are sold around the world, to both countries and insurgencies. Prices vary depending on where the purchases are made and the condition of the weapons. Suffice it to say that low-level weapons are cheap and available. The U.S. State Department says that small arms and light weapons in circulation in 2001 ranged from 100 to 500 million, with 50 to 80 million AK-47s. The AK-47 can be bought in some places for $10 or rented at an hourly rate.[52] At these prices, insurgents like HAMAS and Al Qaeda can procure many weapons. Poorer organization can still get enough at least to start fighting.

The sources for these weapons also vary and make tracking traffic difficult. Governments can supply insurgents directly. Governments in the cold war used to supply insurgencies through other nations. The United States, for instance, used Pakistan to supply the Northern Alliance in Afghanistan.[53] Organized crime can act as a broker. Also, former Soviet military personnel are becoming brokers for arms and other equipment. One such officer supplied arms to both the Northern Alliance and the Taliban in Afghanistan.[54] It is also possible to get weapons "second hand." These second-generation sources exist as weapons originally sold to people for other conflicts and circulated to second parties beyond that conflict either when it is over or during the conflict.[55]

It is unclear if the weapons dictate the operations or the operations dictate which weapons should be bought. Recall the operations listed in Chapter 3. They largely consisted of infantry combat, bombings, ambush, and kidnapping. Insurgents avoid open battlefield conflict with conventional forces, and the fights center around cities. The weapons used seem tailored to the operations described in advantageous locations for the insurgents. Cities are also marketplaces. This allows for direct conduits to buying more weapons and replenishing weapons and ammunition that have been destroyed or used up. Cities also necessitate short-range weapons (alleviating the long-range precision weapon advantage of the more advanced militaries). This makes small arms and light weaponry more effective than they would be on an open battlefield. Cities also provide a cover and concealment that are better not only for warfare, but also for the transfer of weapons and the access to them. Population congestion inside cities also tends to make the weapons insurgents use more deadly.

Another facet of procurement is that research and development are less imperative. Insurgents buy weapons made by governments, which means they buy finished products. Governments spend money on invention and improvement of their own weaponry; insurgents do not. That is not to say that insurgents do not innovate. Their innovation is done in battle, not in the laboratory, which means insurgents do not pay the costs governments pay for producing new weapons. They simply pay the cost to buy finished products. They can make their own amendments to the weapons they possess, with the amendments born of necessity in battle; this also means that it happens quicker and without the cost of the infrastructure involved.

Ultimately, the weapons procured are the most effective ones for the type of warfare in which insurgents use weapons. Their chosen weapons are cheap, plentiful, and effective in the context of the operations and politics involved. They are usable by amateurs, with minimal training.

Training

Training allows soldiers to take action effectively under fire. Better training makes forces more effective. That training comes in the form of information and practice. Information refers to what can be learned by reading, watching, and lecture. That information is relatively easy to get, perhaps as easy as going to amazon.com, and finding U.S. Army field manuals or books on explosives and demolitions, which exist there, among many other places on the Internet. Information is important. The more you learn the better you think and the more able you are to build or advance new ways of doing things as necessity and inspiration strike. But, information cannot stand alone; thinking is not doing.

Practice is also important. Practice allows knowledge to be used practically. Indeed, practice allows knowledge to be married to action. More than that, practice develops in the individual a presence of mind and follow-through in both professional soldiers and insurgents, who use knowledge to take action under pressure, an essential ingredient for engaging in combat. Thus, all training for war needs both classrooms and training camps and is also why simulations are becoming more and more popular. Simulations are a way of training decision makers to put their knowledge to use in practical circumstances. The combination of information and practice also serves to divulge efficiency and best practices for various actions. This works best when it takes counsel of experiences garnered from previous actions and operations. Experience changes knowledge and training, making better practices and better fighters as a result.

Training may have different aims for insurgent fighters than for professional soldiers. Professional soldiers need to have standard operating procedures. Armies need to have soldiers working all "on the same page" and require high levels of excellence. This form of discipline is necessary for soldiers of large conventional armies because those armies depend on soldiers in the field knowing their duty and doing it. Conventional armies depend on soldiers being capable of taking orders from a variety of officers and carrying those orders out under fire. Insurgents, on the other hand, do not seem to need the same things. It seems to be more important to make sure that training gives insurgents the ability to be effective at what they do. This becomes especially important for insurgents isolated and distributed in various places around the world, where interchangeability is less of a possibility and self-sufficiency becomes a much more desirable quality. Insurgents still need discipline, but the training for this kind of discipline is not as involved as the training of professional soldiers. There is less to learn and less formality involved in the learning for insurgents.

What goes into training? Basic topics are probably tackled: funding, politics, infiltration, operations, observation, and recruiting. Carrying out actions in each of those topics requires practice; even for insurgents, those practices require facilities for training. Again, the training has a different flavor. Insurgents do not seem to train as part of an army. Instead, they train as small units, cells, or even individuals.[56] Not only now but also in ages past, insurgents have not gone through the same sort of formal training as professionals. In many cases, they received training simply by surviving one battle after another. The more battles they survived, the more "training" they got. Insurgent training is also not so much about discipline as it is about endurance or survival. Their training is not complex or expensive. It may not be as good as what professional soldiers receive, but it may not need to be.

Instruction can take place through a variety of media. There has never been a better time for the dissemination of information. Books, Web sites, multimedia, document sharing, faxes, and videoconferencing are all available for the dissemination of information. Contrast this with 30 years ago, when only books were available and whatever other printed media could be had by one insurgency or another. Implications of the information age for insurgency today are numerous.

Information can be easily replicated, stored, and communicated to many people at the same time over and over again. The equipment for transmitting and receiving that information is plentiful, and people can get and use the equipment easily.

There is also wider access to regular schools, where training can be received in various practical topics. Developing a system for educating insurgents is largely a question of deciding the best methods for getting the information across. It could be by reading, lecture, Web sites, distance learning classes, or training camps. Heightened access to information becomes a catalyst for delivering training to insurgents.

The instruction can actually take place every day. The knowledge is all around and is useful to society beneficially. Because the information is useful to society, it is made accessible to all. But, any information can be turned to darkness. Learning how to build or how to do contains in it learning how to destroy. Institutions exist all over the world that contain this knowledge. For instance, one could go to college and there learn engineering, biology, chemistry, or computer science. Learning about those topics, one can learn to engage in demolitions and about explosives, diseases, poison, and the sabotage of people and infrastructure. One could join an army, and there learn about firearms, organization, tactics, and explosives. One could go to a trade school and learn to be an electrician, plumber, computer programmer, truck driver, or airplane pilot. This is not something that only happens in this country. Information is available worldwide in one way or another. This makes it possible for insurgents to go to a country, obtain the information needed for operations, assimilate into the country, and start operations there. This sort of education is available every day. The knowledge is not only easily acquired, but also easily shared, and transferral of information by word of mouth is multiplied many times over by the Internet. Classroom learning in its benign form can be done every day in the open.

Illegal acts, on the other hand, particularly using bullets and bombs, also need practice. The difficulty is that for insurgents the practice cannot be done in the open, which is why secret training camps exist. That fact means training is probably less formal and regimented than what conventional armies receive. It means innovation takes place in the field, not in the lab as discussed in the preceding section, and is brought to the training camp. The training camp is the place where that newly gained information is divulged. This is probably how car bombs became suicide bombs and improved explosive devices detonated by cell phone or garage door opener started.

A troubling aspect of this everyday access to knowledge and training is that, unknowingly, we engage in this training for our enemies.

Oklahoma City bomber Timothy McVeigh was trained in the U.S. Army. To go back a few decades, Admiral Yamamoto, the architect of the Pearl Harbor raid, studied at Harvard. Of course, the September 11 hijackers learned how to fly planes in the United States. This is not a testament against open education, although obviously some care should be taken about who gets the education. It is meant to show that it is often not possible to know the ends of education. Information is not good or evil in and of itself. Once the knowledge is gained, it is easy to corrupt it and even easier in this day and age to teach it to others.

Taking the knowledge gained and teaching others is also the point at which training camps come into play. Based on jihadist training camp notebooks, it is possible to see the curriculum given to insurgents. Many often take that training back to where they came from to train others.[57] In these notebooks, insurgents are taught map reading and the use of small arms.[58] They are also taught about targeting, both on the ground and in the air, as well as explosives and demolitions.[59] Interestingly, not only military subjects are taught in these camps. Insurgents learn that all goals must be mutually reinforcing, and propaganda is important as a part of the action. This is a different way of combat from Western ideas of war. In this case, the combat is connected intimately to politics and religion and can be so for other issues as well.[60]

Learning in a training camp is obviously task oriented. The teachers, like drill sergeants in professional armies all over the world, teach from practical experience. Volunteers, on the other hand, bring a pot-luck aspect to training camps; that is, they have varying motivation and offer varying quality when they enter training. Training camps are also good places to find the best insurgents. Just as training camps in professional armies yield the best soldiers, those better insurgents in some cases are offered the chance to take part in larger efforts.[61]

In these ways, camp is better than the classroom. It is not possible to learn violence in a basement without drawing attention. It is also not possible to learn how to be efficient in using violence by practicing for an hour twice a week. This type of learning requires usage of skills to use and maintain weapons. Isolation helps trainees focus and makes indoctrination easier through immersion. In the end, camps culminate information into something useful to the movement. Information is important but not in and of itself. It must feed the movement. The training is not as formal or involved as in professional armies. The standards are not the same. The training is still undeniably effective, and the results of that training testify in blood in incidents all over the world. Effectiveness is tied to simplicity, marrying tactical action with global context. Tactical action means using cells or other small units in small-scale operations, such as bombing and ambush. The type of warfare discussed here not only requires less complexity for the actions taken, but also requires more political complexity to be sure that the tasks support the agenda advanced. Selecting targets is not simply military. The targets must be both vulnerable and politically useful to the movement.

Professional militaries exist in the open and are able to protect themselves; insurgent forces do not and cannot. They must learn to sustain themselves as a dispersed body. They must learn to maintain connections to other groups to survive, and they must do so while infiltrated in a target society. This requires a very different type of training from that of professional forces.

Part of the effectiveness of insurgent training is the lack of complexity needed. Knowledge and practice are more available without high-tech weapons and large forces. Coupled with small infrastructure needs, this means that training can be done in many places and can be constituted and reconstituted where and when needed. The key to this is that the knowledge is more important than the infrastructure. As long as the knowledge survives to be transferred, the system is never dead. This poses a problem for counterinsurgency forces. If the training system cannot be destroyed when its infrastructure is destroyed and the multiplicity of possibilities for transmitting the information mean that transmission also cannot be fully destroyed, how is it possible to disrupt the training system? It may come down to destroying the teachers who deliver the information. Even this may not work if others are capable of stepping into their places. Simplicity works, especially when it is backed by initiative and dedication.

This kind of training can be a prolific creator of insurgents. It teaches simple things quickly, cheaply, and with less investment. In the context of insurgency war for issue-related goals, this makes it very effective. Training can sprout formally or informally in a number of places. The implications of this are the possibilities of indoctrinating and training large numbers of people using an overall system of political education for training fighters worldwide. It is a system of identifying and training cadres to lead a global effort. The system asks commitment and sacrifice and shows insurgents how to do it in a relevant way. It does not require complexity or formality of them, which is part of its appeal and its effectiveness. The system can be destroyed and reconstituted quickly. The same cannot be said of professional training systems. If, for instance, the United States lost aspects of its training system because they are tied to infrastructure dependence, it would be very hard to rebuild them.

The main weakness of an insurgent training system as described here is that it requires attendance to be successful. If truancy could be made to happen on a large enough scale, then that would probably be the downfall of the system. Insurgencies probably have difficulty enforcing truancy because of lack of resources. They depend on dedication, among other things, to perpetuate themselves.

Conclusion

Support for war as described here mimics what governments do. The scale is not as big and the results are not competitive with what governments do, but it is effective, and what is more, this system is capable of being camouflaged from the eyes of national governments and international organizations. There is a very small infrastructure footprint, instead piggybacking on established systems or utilizing those systems with less formality. Because precision, overtness, and transparency are less important to insurgencies, there is less need for large numbers, heavy equipment, or large buildings. These things also do not fit in with insurgency operations and their attending politics. The point is that it is possible to construct global systems for wealth, acquisition, and training to support and sustain a global insurgency.

It is important to remember that these systems are not in direct competition with governments. They should not be judged in direct comparison with governments. Doing so creates the illusion of scale as superiority, which has proved costly in the past. Insurgencies do not compete by scale but by context. That is, comparing these insurgencies directly with governments and noting how small they look next to governments tends to minimize their ability to engage in operations.

The size and comparative scale are not the point. The ability to be effective in context is the point. It is probably better to judge whether an insurgency can be effective on its own on a scale necessary to support itself. The evidence of the past 20 years, particularly in the Middle East, seems to point to the answer being that it can. Insurgencies today seem to be carving new niches from untapped markets ignored by larger entities. Anyone in business today can understand the significance of that idea. Support systems can be effective in feeding other parts of the insurgency, and the effectiveness of those other parts feeds the support network. September 11th was not simply a military or even a political victory for Al Qaeda. It also fed recruit-ing, funding, and training.

The systems viewed here are not unlike a virus feeding off a host. As the virus feeds, it becomes stronger. The host, on the other hand, weakens. As the host gets weaker, the virus replicates. Soon, the virus dominates its host and after a time communicates itself to new hosts. The only way to stop it is to change the conditions under which it can flourish. Insurgency support can also be stunted but not so much by tactical action as by changing the conditions that make the support effective.

Chapter 6

A THEORY OF GLOBAL INSURGENCY

Thus far, discussion has centered on observable phenomena. Each chapter has recounted evidence of the availability of the components of war to every human being. It is not enough simply to describe what exists. It is better to deliver some meaning to what we see. If we know what the evidence means when it is put together, we can do useful things with it. We can know what it is and is not. We can use it as a tool for analysis and planning. We can see what possibilities lie ahead. There is no point in describing this information if it cannot be used to help.

Understanding Global Insurgency

Some things about the global insurgency type of war do not change. This is still the fulfillment of an agenda through violence. It is still necessary to gather resources to support the effort. It still requires training of people to perform tasks. Funding must be collected for the effort. Intelligence must be collected, analyzed, and processed. People must be mobilized. These things must be done in all wars, in all ages, no matter the form or the goal.

That said, this type of warfare has much to it that differs from other wars. The overall character of global insurgency is different. Much about it is not formal or permanent. For example, the infrastructure, composition, and tempo of operations, as we have seen, are quite different from conventional warfare. Indeed, a global insurgency can change, subtly or not, from week to week. The same services are used as in conventional warfare, but the character of the services is different. Conventional warfare is more constant; insurgency is less so.

Agenda setting has changed. Power comes from inclusion of people, not acquisition of territory. It drives the choice of action to insurgencies. It is composed by agreement, not dictation. It is meant to attract followers as much as guide planning and action. Because the agenda is used to advance transnational issues, it can attract a global following.

Violence has changed. Localized violence is made in a variety of places. It is not massed in a single place. Political violence is done not only by professional soldiers but also by amateurs. The operations themselves are simple, not complex. The violence emphasizes political and nonmilitary results. Insurgents seek coverage of expanding areas rather than concentration in one area.

Mobilization has changed. The people involved may be evangelists for their cause, not simply volunteers or conscripts. The difference is worth noting. It is in some cases the difference between someone who volunteers to fight and someone who volunteers to blow him- or herself up and kill as many of the enemy as possible at the same time. They are dedicated to the cause in that way. Yet at the same time, their dedication is not constant in its tempo. They come, and they go. They are not always actively working for the cause necessarily, just when they must.

Gathering resources has changed. Contributions come from those who can contribute and are delivered to those with need. Resources are not amassed in plenty; they are amassed in enough quantity to meet the need when possible. Resources expand and contract with the ebb and flow of the issue. This is in contrast to how governments handle these things, amassing large numbers of resources in terms of people and talent as well as material and keeping a large amount of stock on hand.

Intelligence has changed. Collection is done locally and serves both local and global needs. It is decentralized, so it has a quicker turnover to become useful. This is in contrast with large intelligence organizations that are centralized and therefore much slower. Over time, centralized intelligence is more accurate and more comprehensive but much slower.

Funding has changed. We have seen that it has become possible to use funding systems outside the regular financial systems that the governments of the world use and advocate. These outside systems are less permanent and less trackable. They operate on a smaller scale at which all forms of tender are used and can be converted back and forth easily. This makes it easier for people operating outside the conventional world still to be able to fund their efforts.

For all of these differences from conventional war, global insurgency is possible. It does work. It can be effective, as Al Qaeda illustrates. That is, although global insurgencies can operate very differently and on a level that compared head to head cannot compete with what governments do, they can still be effective.

Global insurgency can be visualized better with a model. A model is a template or construct showing the relation of components and how they work together to produce results. It can be represented by a diagram or an explanation; we will do both. If we can make it tangible and give it form and substance, it will help us understand what we have been talking about. We can draw conclusions from it, and those conclusions will help us know what we are seeing and how to use it or how to defeat it.

Figure 6.1 shows a grouping of organizations, each with their own characteristics. It works in this way. The issue attracts a number of organizations seeking to advance an agenda. Member groups

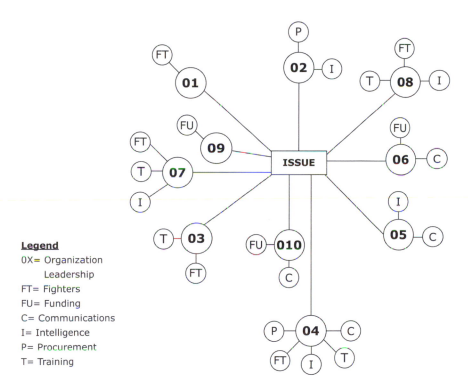

Figure 6.1 Global insurgency model

convene to define goals and craft a message. Members combine in various ways and contribute their services to the cause. Members coordinate their efforts with each other to craft a message and agenda. Members take actions, which connect to other issues. Membership expands or contracts with the results of those actions, and the cycle repeats.

Note that the organizations have different characteristics. Only some members fight. Others contribute funds. Still others contribute weapons. One organization cannot do all tasks. No one organization can fill the agenda by itself. Because the members are an eclectic group, each can contribute its unique skills. Together, they combine in various ways to cover everything that needs to be covered. The issue is the glue that holds the organizations together. These are the physical traits of the model.

There are also nonphysical characteristics. The politics of the issue hold sway over the actions taken. This differs from conventional warfare, in which attempts are often made to divorce politics from action. The insurgency draws strength from inclusiveness. It is more eclectic in views, in decision making, and in solutions. It is a grass-roots movement and gives the whole insurgency local advantages (knowledge of locations, resource availability, etc.). Wherever it has a group component located, these local advantages transfer to the whole membership. Because the insurgency is global, it is always able to find weakness somewhere as a result. It never allows decisive action to be taken against the whole. It cannot be destroyed by decapitation. It is thin, wiry, and slight, but strong in its own way. It depends on people more than physical infrastructure or institutions for its strength. So, if this is what global insurgency looks like and acts like, what does it do? It produces gains in popular support. The support makes the issue more important. Importance makes the insurgency powerful, and that power allows them to advance their agenda worldwide.

The five previous chapters yield to us the characteristics of a global insurgency, which can be condensed into a template that allows us to recognize what global insurgency looks like and what it does. It can help explain what the insurgency is about and what its goals are. It can help predict generally what the insurgency will do to gain its ends. The template has the following characteristics:

1. The insurgency generates services like governments to fight wars.
2. The insurgency seeks popular support.
3. Global insurgencies are composed of diverse groups connected in multiple locations.

4. The insurgency is connected and motivated by an issue.
5. The issue attracts many organizations with related, sympathetic concerns.
6. The attractiveness of the issue feeds the connections that make for global power.
7. The insurgency can coordinate action in multiple places.
8. The insurgency can take actions in multiple places.
9. The actions of the insurgents connect directly to the issue or cause.
10. The insurgency uses all tools to advance the issue and grow its power.

Any movement observed to have these characteristics may (depending on its goals) be a global insurgency.

If the global insurgency is succeeding, the following things may happen: The issue rises in importance in a number of places. Governments perceive the weight of the issue and address it by either supporting it or opposing it. The behavior of anything related to the issue changes. The government's agenda and other issues are supplanted, forestalled, or reduced.

With this template, we now have the means to understand global insurgency at least a little bit. We can recognize it and know how it works. We can know what it is after, and we can know how it achieves success. Even that is not enough to truly understand it. We must set global insurgency in some kind of context. That way, we can try to see where it fits in with conventional wisdom and know its limits. To achieve that, a number of "frequently asked questions" are explored next. The aim of these questions is to further define the phenomenon through a question-and-answer process. This engages us in a discussion of what global insurgency is and is not. We can look at how effective insurgency can be. We can also see what limits it has. We can note why it is considered new and what future it might have.

Frequently Asked Questions

How Effective Can Insurgency Be?

Insurgency can be very effective in the proper context. It takes advantage of conventional warfare's weaknesses while it enhances its own strengths. The art of war was not constructed so the strong may conquer. It was constructed so the weak can defend against the strong. This is particularly true of insurgency. Insurgents avoid battle because battle might destroy them. Instead, they destroy things the conventional armies need to be effective. This strategy works anywhere if it is used correctly.

The effectiveness is enhanced when attacking infrastructure. Infrastructure is needed for efficiently running an economy. It is also needed to run a military efficiently, particularly when it depends on high technology and heavy logistics. Indeed, such armies and such economies are highly dependent right now on physical infrastructure, and that infrastructure is everywhere. What is more, the infrastructure usually is very delicate and not able to withstand attack.

It is possible to engage in insurgency on a wide scale because it does not require concentration of forces to make an attack. The example of the French Resistance support of the D Day invasion most closely resembles what a modern global insurgency might look like. In this example, small teams of 10 to 20 people fanned out across an entire country and destroyed infrastructure in an attempt to paralyze or even cripple a conventional army. It happened quickly. It was done with the support of the indigenous population and had the desired effect. There are other examples, for instance, guerrilla activity in the American Civil War in the South and, of course, T. E. Lawrence and the Arab revolt in World War I. But, for the type of insurgency about which we are talking, the French Resistance is probably the best example of what we see now and in the future. Today, we are even more dependent on infrastructure for economic and military activity than we have ever been, and that dependence enhances the potential effectiveness of insurgent tactics.

Insurgency is also effective because of the political aspects. Insurgencies amass many small successes on a daily basis. Each one relates to the political agenda. This tends to draw people to support the insurgency. Everyone likes a winner. If you hear every day of how the insurgency has destroyed something or killed people, it begins to reinforce in the minds of the general population that the insurgency is successful, and that they might win. People begin looking to be on the winning side and throw their support more and more to the insurgency. That support helps the movement grow and allows for even more activities to take place in this day and age. Expansion can even move to other nations.

Why Does Insurgency Create Such Problems for Conventional Forces?

Conventional armies seek each other out and either collide with each other or ambush each other. The results of that fight are meant to settle the issue between governments whether it is with a single battle or a series of battles. When one army can no longer fight, a war is considered over. The key feature here is that armies mass to focus power, and the army that is best at doing that usually wins; this decides the war.

Insurgency has a different approach. Insurgents avoid battle with conventional forces. Indeed, insurgents avoid situations for which the possibility is good that they might lose. They are not looking for decision through battle. Instead, they try to win their decision through support of the people and expansion of the movement. This means attacking where there is no army and dispersing when the attack is over.

Dispersion is a key feature of insurgency. Insurgents disperse where a conventional army tries to mass. The army never has a target and so cannot destroy its enemy in decisive battle. At the same time, a conventional army massing to fight such a battle means that some place is not being covered by the conventional army. Some place is weak and not as well defended. This is a part of what makes insurgents successful in taking advantage of the weaknesses inherent in all government forces. Mass cannot cover dispersal. A dispersed army, on the other hand, is weaker, and dispersion runs counter to the principles of conventional war. Insurgents are also less dependent on formal physical infrastructure for their strength. This means they can destroy physical infrastructure, and that will injure conventional armed forces to a greater degree than it will injure insurgents.

Predicting the outcome of the interaction of insurgency and conventional war turns on two points: Which side can take advantage of the weaknesses of the other? Is the issue in question one that can be settled without winning a decisive battle? The degree to which the second claim is true goes a long way to deciding whether insurgency is capable of winning a conflict. The degree to which one side or the other can take advantage of the first point is the degree to which insurgency will survive long enough to be able to do the second.

How Important Are Group Connections?

Group connections are important but do not always mean the same thing in all cases. In insurgencies, the connections can change often. Seeing them is more like looking at a snapshot of a moment, not a sculpture that is the same forever. The U.S. government has had connections with many people who would prove to be future enemies. Connection is not always indicative of long-term association. Talks take place every day among low-level people in various governments, organizations, and even insurgencies. That is not always evidence of strong connection.

Insurgency connections as presented here flow from an issue that makes the connections situational and contextual. Judging firm connections versus transitory connections is a function of the following characteristics: Look for connections that tend to stand over time. Look for connections that influence the direction of an issue. Look for connections that grow support for the issue. These connections indicate featured performers over momentary bit players. They indicate groups that have a vested interest in seeing things through to the end. These are the more permanent connections and the ones to be aware of as most important. Some connections are transitory or false, and it is possible for them to become noise that obscures the true picture. Indeed, it is very possible for insurgents to build false connections purposely to obscure their real purpose, and there should be awareness of this.

Real connections are important because they show the characteristics of the insurgency. They show the composition of the issue, that is, which pieces of the issue are important, to show how various components of an issue relate to each other and by extension how the proponents of those issue components relate to each other. They also hint at what the proponents of various issues that relate to each other seek, how they might achieve their goals, who might win, and who might stay once goals are achieved.

Is It Really Possible to Be Defeated by Global Insurgency?

War is the servant of politics and political goals. We have seen in places like Vietnam and Afghanistan that losing political goals loses the war regardless of success in battle. Battles and their results are still important, but to be useful they must be made to either serve one's own goals or deny the other side achievement of their goals. Our adversaries will try to do the same if they are smart.

It is possible for some goals to be achieved without winning a battle. Goals could be contingent on other things. Popular support is important to insurgency, and making a good showing sometimes will get that support, even if the battle itself is lost. Indeed, as seen with Gandhi in the Indian independence movement, sometimes civil disobedience is good enough to achieve the goals you want. It is important to orient all thought and action to the issue and achieving the goals that will advance the issue. That means being and doing whatever is required. In some cases, what is required is fighting a battle or even winning a battle. In other cases, this is not always required.

It is worth keeping in mind that fighting and winning battle on battle is not always necessary or desirable. In World War I, the German fleet lost the Battle of Jutland to the British Navy. If the German fleet were utterly destroyed, it would free British ships to support the war in a number of ways. As long as that fleet existed, the British navy had to stay in position as long as the German fleet existed. No subsequent naval battles were fought for the rest of the war. Germany's fleet kept the British Navy busy for the rest of the war without fighting another battle.

Costs also enter into the equation, and it is necessary to be mindful of the costs of fighting a war. By its nature, an insurgency costs less. Insurgencies are built with the idea that this is what you do when you have very little with which to fight. Large costly battles are avoided in insurgency. At the same time, the nature of insurgency, because it destroys material and infrastructure, raises the cost of war to others, particularly if the others are fighting a conventional conflict.

In insurgency, all tools must be used, not just force. This is true for all insurgencies (and counter insurgencies for that matter). Because this is true, one must be careful of the actions taken. In particular, care must be taken that actions meant to help your side do not also help the other side. The trick in insurgencies and counterinsurgencies is to give neither comfort nor ease by your own actions to the enemy.

Why Isn't This Terrorism?

The word *terrorism* is not useful as a definition, and there is no agreement on any definition of it. In fact, it does not help us know our enemy better so that we may defeat them. Some definitions can even be turned back on the accusers. For instance, a definition of terrorism as attacks on civilians could include September 11 and suicide bombing, but someone could turn those definitions also to include the bombings in Dresden, Tokyo, Hiroshima, and Nagasaki. It may seem like semantics, but because part of fighting as or against an insurgency is convincing people to listen to you and agree with what you are saying, choosing a definition of terrorism becomes very important; care must be taken not to choose one that can be turned against you. In particular, this is important when the people that you are trying to convince to support you desperately want to do anything but that.

Terrorism is really about labeling violence legitimate or not legitimate. The actual actions can be legitimate or not, depending on context and point of view. This makes terrorism as a term subjective, and it is a bad idea to base the definition of the enemy subjectively as a prelude to defending against them. It is more useful to call it in-surgency. This term describes the action without subjective judg-ment. It speaks to the actions as they are (ambush, suicide bombing, assassination). These actions define the enemy more accurately. This allows for a better plan of defense against them. It is easier this way to assign meaning to their actions clinically, and it is easier to track enemy behavior and plan a defense.

Calling these actions terrorism also has the added effect of making the insurgencies sound implacable, shrouded in mystery. It is better to demystify them, to define them coldly and accurately, and to come up with a plan to defeat them on that basis. This leads to better un-derstanding of the differences between conventional and insurgency action.

Don't the Experts Say That No One Can Win a War with Insurgency?

Yes, the experts say that no one can win a war with insurgency. They are right in a certain context. All wars are different to a lesser or greater degree, and context sets the stage for winning and losing wars. There are many experts. Chief among them are Clausewitz, Mao, and T. E. Lawrence, who all wrote about insurgency. It should be noted that they wrote to their own time and their own experience. Clausewitz wrote about a war of big armies fighting for possession of land in the Napoleonic age. Mao wrote about liberating China from Japanese occupation during World War II. Lawrence wrote about Arab revolt on the Arabian Peninsula during World War I. Some of what they say still holds true, but because of context and the passage of time, some does not.

We should examine what they say in context. Clausewitz did preach concentration of force for decisive action.[1] Yet, he also recognized the worth of the guerrillas (insurgents) of Spain. He knew that such forces must never concentrate, or they would be crushed.[2] He did see guer-rillas as primarily an adjunct to main national efforts.[3] Mao also be-lieved that insurgents must either become conventional armies or act in support of them.[4] As someone who actually conducted insurgency for years before taking power, Mao understood both the importance of popular support and the need to make force serve a political agenda to be successful.[5] In context, Mao was trying to take over and rule China.

Finally, there was T. E. Lawrence or, as many people know him, Lawrence of Arabia. Lawrence reasoned that conventional warfare would not work for the Arab revolt.[6] He recognized that doing so would make the Turkish forces engage in the kind of trench warfare going on in Europe at that time.[7] Instead, he wondered what the Turkish army would do if the Arab revolt was an insurgency, "an idea" instead of an army, giving no target to Turkish soldiers.[8] He knew that a war in which popular support was as necessary as bullets would have a much better chance of success.[9]

All three writers saw the power of insurgency. Their pronouncements on how it can be used to fight still ring true today. Their pronouncements on the ultimate ends of insurgency are contextual to their times. None could foresee what it would look like in the context of today's world. What has not changed is that insurgency still allows the weak to survive long enough to grow and gain power. At the same time, if they grew into a conventional army as Mao suggested, they would lose, especially today, to most conventional armed forces. Instead, they grow issue support in as many places around the world as possible. If they get more people to support them, they become more powerful. Figure that in these terms: If you can get more people to support your version of the truth, you become stronger. Get them to vote your way to get them to govern your way. Get them to think and act your way. In today's world, that is a win. It is as much about politics, connectivity, and inclusiveness as it is about the use of force.

What Are the Limits of Global Insurgency?

Global insurgency is slow and takes time to build into something useful. Because it is not a nation-state, resources must be built and not levied. Because part of the object is convincing people to follow, it means tying the movement to a very slow and uncertain process. Insurgency seeks no immediate decision, so it can survive long enough to expand. It means there will be no quick, decisive action.

Insurgency relies on politics, not force, for decision. This means that its gains will be less quantifiable, and so there will be less indication of where things stand day to day. Issues have an ebb and flow of salience and support. This means that on any given day, you might be a little closer to or a little further away from winning. The indicators of success change after each interaction with supporters and opponents. In short, there is no one milestone plan for getting there. Insurgent victory may resemble waking up one morning and finding that it has happened.

Insurgency is not decisive because there are no large battles. You need the other side's acquiescence to win, and as stated, it is not always clear who is winning on any given day. It is hard to communicate being on the right track. The main indicator is popular support. This is a less quantifiable and not necessarily reliable measurement of how a war is going. In some instances, that support will take the form of a vocal and active minority, and in others the support will be from a larger but less-vocal and active population. People will say what they think others want to hear, particularly if the threat of violence is in the air. In short, because there is no decisive action, there is no clear way of knowing where things stand on either side.

Insurgencies are fragile. They make do with what they have, which at first is not much. They cannot protect themselves from armies if they are out in the open. So, they engage in a lot of hiding. Because insurgencies depend on popular support, they suffer from variable loyalty. This problem must constantly be tended, or the popular support drops. It can mean setbacks to all insurgency efforts.

It is important to keep track of assessed limits. The limits hold the keys to defeating global insurgency. Insurgents rely on different things than governments do. Defeating them means vigilance, attendance to politics, focus, and gaining support from people as well as the use of violence.

Can Insurgents Take Over a Country or the World?

Insurgents probably cannot take over lands and people in a conventional way. Nationalism is still a powerful connector of people. Trying to take over a nation evokes that nationalism. In appealing to German nationalism, Hitler proved that the reverse is possible with the support of a nation. Remember that the Nazis helped other Nazi parties to form in other German-speaking countries, and those Nazi parties helped the Nazis and Germans in Germany assimilate those countries into the Third Reich.

On the other hand, insurgencies can take over issues that appeal to small groups in a way that can circumvent nationalism. If they are not perceived as affecting nationalism, issues can appeal to individual but shared concerns. That is, they can appeal to things that do not involve nationalism, like religion or health care. Those are concerns of individuals or small groups in a given country. If there are people or groups like that in every country, the issue becomes more important, taking over an issue and possibly making it a global insurgency.

The issue again appeals to individual but shared concerns. If insurgents can command a popular point of view on an issue, then they can have power in one nation or in a number of nations where people who share their concern also share the point of view. If that happens, then it is possible to get people to vote, think, and act according to the insurgents' point of view, and that represents the power to infiltrate and subvert governments.

Governments also live on popular support, and this infiltration can create difficulties. If the insurgency is able to do this, then it is not a physical takeover but a political one. Again, this was something seen with Hitler's hijacking of German nationalism in the 1930s. It is not an insurgency in the conventional sense, but the Nazis did have followers in other nations help assimilate people to the cause and pave the way for the fall of a number of European governments. This works best when it is an issue that nobody is directly against. Al Qaeda is doing something like this today.

Is This Suggesting That War Has Been Replaced by Bloodless Conflict?

This is not to suggest that war has been replaced by bloodless conflict. There will still be violence, but it is now subject to timing and context. As an analogy, think of boxers and the tempo of their fighting. A very quick boxer might use flurries of punches to wear an opponent down. A very strong fighter might stalk the ring, taking great swings in hopes of getting a knockout. Some fighters, on the other hand, will simply wait for an opening to strike while trying to avoid punishment. The same principles apply to warfare.

All fighting has a tempo. Conventional armies campaign. Campaigning can take the form of constant warfare or at least constant contact with the enemy.[10] Insurgents, on the other hand, try to pick a moment to strike. Those moments may come every day, or they may be few and far between. Insurgencies take a number of small actions that add up. We are seeing it today in Iraq, a conflict that is certainly not bloodless. It seems like the small actions are less or amount to less because governments do things like the Normandy invasion. But, governments also can fight like insurgents if needed.

What is going on now is violence directly serving politics. It used to be that violence was used to decide politics. Armies would fight, and the decision produced from the fighting would be interpreted as deciding political goals. That was the conventional warfare model evolving from a philosophy of total war for total victory, which was the hallmark of wars in the 19th and 20th centuries. Now, we are beginning to see aspects of what Joseph Nye called "soft power" becoming important. Now, conflict is not just about the use of force. According to Nye, using power is also about who we can get to agree with us and who currently agrees with the other side.[11] Nye recognized that nongovernmental organizations possess this power as much as governments do and are capable of building coalitions for their issues.[12] Fighting this type of war requires a different mindset about force and other tools that might be useful.

Can These Issues Obtain Global Support?

Many issues can obtain global support. Think of issues any given person might support. Imagine that those issues are opposed or ignored by your government. You could find the support of like-minded people in your community or other communities worldwide. If you and the like-minded connect and act together, it means that your issue now has global support. There are many benign examples of this, such as Amnesty International or Doctors Without Borders.

This is a simple answer, but the reality is more complex. Not every popular issue leads to global action. Not every issue gives power or breeds violence. Issues can range from those that have an effect on long-term futures (such as the future of Islam, globalization, or environment) to other issues (health care, trade) that have not so far.

Gladwell's *The Tipping Point* gives an indicator of how these things happen. Gladwell researched how social things like television shows and social trends go from being little known to being widely known and adopted. He asserted that sometimes power comes from having large number of acquaintances, allowing new ideas to be transmitted to large numbers of people, who in turn may adopt the ideas and transmit them to others.[13] Starting such an epidemic is a matter of finding a way to translate new ideas to the masses in a way that allows them to digest and adopt them.[14] One way of doing this is to create communities to reinforce those beliefs.[15] Simply put, it requires people with knowledge of what is going on, people with connections who can spread the word, and a context in which everyone is open to obtaining the information and using it.[16] Issues that affect the long-term future with these three characteristics may become future insurgencies.

Can All of These Small, Single Actions Really Gain Larger Results?

The small, single actions themselves are raids and ambushes. They feed a strategy of growing one's own side while weakening the enemy. In this way, tactical actions take on much larger importance. There is a tendency to downplay the results of small-scale actions. This goes back to the idea that insurgencies cannot win wars. It is possible to take tactical action with strategic results. For example, a squad of 10 soldiers could be sent to kill someone. If they kill another soldier, the result is tactical; it has a local effect. On the other hand, if the single person that they kill is a head of state, that has a much larger effect and is probably more strategic. This is not to say that taking such an action could win a war. The context of the action decides its reach and its importance.

By way of example, consider the career of Nazi commando Otto Skorzeny. During World War II, Skorzeny recaptured Benito Mussolini from the Allies, forestalling a full Italian surrender for many months. The simple act of kidnapping him from his guards changed the plans of the Allies immensely. Skorzeny actually did this again, kidnapping the son of the Hungarian regent to stop Hungary's surrender to the Soviet Union, keeping Hungary in the war on the German side until the very end. It is interesting to note that after the war Skorzeny was a consultant to the government of Egypt and trained Palestinian fighters in unconventional warfare.[17]

One of the hallmarks of Skorzeny's operations was taking advantage of the standard operating procedures of conventional forces in using raids and surprise to do great damage with relatively small operations.[18] He was a great innovator, always using unconventional methods to achieve success. He trained English-speaking German soldiers on how to be like American soldiers so they could impersonate Americans behind their lines in the Battle of the Bulge.[19] These impostors successfully created chaos in the American rear areas, changing road signs and cutting phone lines.[20] He also worked on modifying the V-1 rocket to be piloted.[21] Later, he also worked on the possibility of launching those weapons from submarines, possibly at America.[22]

In a way, Skorzeny was the intellectual godfather of September 11, although it is unclear how direct his influence was on current Middle Eastern insurgencies. The point here is not to dismiss small actions and their value without knowing the context in which they are made. The example of Otto Skorzeny shows it is very possible for small-scale actions like bombings, ambushes, and kidnappings to have far-reaching repercussions.

Is This to Say That Amateur Insurgents Can Beat Professional Soldiers?

This is hardly to say that amateur insurgents can be professional soldiers. Insurgents cannot withstand professional soldiers. This is warfare in which victory is taken through politics. It is not about beating armies; it is about feeding issues to gather support to grow power. Political leadership decides what the results of battles mean. Remember that the Nazis did not surrender until Hitler died. France under Napoleon did not surrender until Waterloo; the North Vietnamese did not win a major battle in their war with America, and yet they never surrendered. In war, commitment and staying power play their part as much as force does.

Professionals have a resilience that allows politicians to stay committed. It takes a lot of defeat to end a war fought conventionally. Amateurs have an ebb and flow of resiliency. In other words, they are not constant, and their physical resilience is not predictable. That makes it hard to know if it is really possible to win with insurgency day to day, but the distributed nature of insurgents, coupled with their ability to hide, gives them a "soft resiliency." Their real resiliency comes from support people give to the insurgent issue.

Amateurs should not be dismissed. Fighting can be learned and experience can be gained by amateurs. The school of hard knocks sometimes teaches as well as military academies. That is why it is not unheard of for barroom brawlers to defeat trained martial artists. It is also why in the English Civil War Oliver Cromwell helped form the New Model Army, was able to defeat the Royalists, and became the dictator of Great Britain with no formal military training.[23]

Amateurs are an unknown commodity. They do not have the same quality or reliability as professionals. They do have other qualities that work. Even being undisciplined and erratic can be useful in a world that expects order and recoils from chaos. Amateurs will not be able to destroy the U.S. armed forces or most other armies on the planet, but they can be good enough to have a global influence that cannot be ignored.

Why Is This Happening Now?

We can propose three major factors why this is happening now (there are probably more): political openness, globalism, and access. Openness refers to discovering and embracing new political ideas once thought dangerous (like democracy). The fall of communism lifted the prohibitions on new political ideas. After that, it was no longer important to crush proponents of those ideas with internal security forces. There was no justification for not trying new ideas. There was no balance of power to be defended. This left people looking for undefined alternatives to fill the vacuum communism's fall created.

Globalism brings Western economics to the world. Although it has been beneficial to a number of people, the perception is that it has not been beneficial to all, and some perceive that it imposes boundaries. It is undeniably a path to wealth and power, but it also creates a disaffected population who fear the effects of globalization on their lives. These disaffected people either cannot or will not participate, and that means they either have not or will not reap the rewards of the system. They instead feel called on to oppose it with their own issues.

Access is the egalitarianism of giving people the means to power. This gives them information on issues, other people's views, and which actions are being taken in other places. It allows one to find people who can help, fight, teach, or find whatever is necessary to advance an issue. It gives one tools to connect, share, and grow a movement. The confluence of these three factors at this same time bring the changes that we see. The absence of one or more of these factors probably means that no change would have taken place.

What Conditions Are Created by the Change?

In the post-Communist world, governments of all types decided making money was good. In search of Western economic success, many of these nations have courted Western ideas of producing wealth and have been influenced by Western culture. Some issues are not addressed if they run counter to this pursuit. This makes people who find these issues important feel left out. Those who are left out wonder if others are also feeling left out, and they begin a search for them. Their search brings them to seek out capable, like-minded people so they can gather and see what might be done to help themselves.

This is a dynamic of human history. All human history can be couched in terms of a search for and connection with like people followed by gathering together with them. However, when they found someone who was different, they tried either to assimilate them or to destroy them. The connection brings growth, and the failure of connection brings death. This is the process by which humanity defines friends and enemies. So it is here in the 21st century with building global support for an issue.

The openness of world politics brings the greatest change. It allows ideas to germinate in many places. This fact means a faction might be crushed in one nation but not in all nations. This means that force alone cannot destroy ideas in an open world. Global economics cause the ideas and issues to surface. The open system allows the opportunity to grow, and access is the catalyst that brings cohesion to the movement.

Isn't Information Technology the Real Driver of Global Insurgency?

On the surface, it may seem like information technology is the real driver of global insurgency. It is a catalyst; it allows global connection and information exchange. It makes movements global and cohesive yet cannot carry issues alone. Real global insurgency is about people. If people were universally satisfied with the direction the world is going, there would be no insurgency like that of Al Qaeda. Conversely, if people refused to get involved and make contributions, there would be no global insurgency. Such is not the case; people are active, and they are dissatisfied.

People use the tool to gain power. This sort of egalitarian empowerment is not new. A case can be made that gunpowder was given to the masses in the West to make Western armies more effective. Having access to knowledge and the tools of power, allowed Western peoples to surge ahead of their counterparts in the East. Masses with the knowledge of power began to seek power for themselves, and their search for power produced representative government and free markets. Eastern nations, on the other hand, withheld gunpowder from the masses, and they fell behind. The repercussions of this seem to define the developed and the underdeveloped world. Today, information technology is getting into the hands of the masses, and it is pulling power away from governments.

The more important idea is that representative governments and free market economies were sought by empowered people. Gunpowder was a tool. It brought about the transition from government by elites to government by representatives. The possession of information technology may help people gain power and transition from representative government to populist politics and populist war. Empowered people are advancing their own politics. They use issue-based organizations and issue-based forces to try to fulfill their will.

Haven't the Issues People Are Advancing Always Been Around?

The issues people are advancing have always been around, and people have always fought about them. This will continue. The issues of poverty, equality, food, water, and tradition are all future issues of constant salience. They are not new. What is new is people advancing these issues on a global level using violence and contending with governments on a global level. Even doing it on a national level has only been going on for a century or two.

How Long Will These Global Insurgencies Be a Threat?

Global insurgencies will be a threat as long as conditions that support insurgencies exist. If governments either ignore or oppose issues people think are vital, insurgencies will continue. If people can connect to each other and act to advance issues, they will continue. Governments can change these conditions by either including people or denying them access. People can change these conditions by acquiescence to the way things are or choosing not to participate. There are good outcomes and bad outcomes associated with changing these conditions. They are a product of using good or bad methods to make the changes.

Bad methods change conditions with adverse effects. Governments can exclude popular issues, perpetuating the rise of insurgency. Governments can deny people access to the world, but that will harm global economics. People, on the other hand, can drop out and try to live outside the world system that now exists, but that will be a hard existence for them, and it will not solve their problems.

Good methods can change conditions with beneficial effects. For instance, governments could include issue group agendas in their plans, exchanging some power and legitimacy for not having an insurgency. On the other hand, people could emphasize civil disobedience, although it should be noted that such actions work best on benevolent governments rather than oppressive ones.

Some methods will change the conditions quickly but yield adverse outcomes. For instance, governments could cut popular access for people to learn and connect on an issue. They can deny them participation for their issue in government agendas. These methods will change the conditions quickly and probably end global insurgencies. But, they will also damage the world economy, and it will be expensive to shut those things down.

Some methods will change very little and prolong conditions for global insurgency. In other words, governments could allow maintaining access for people to connect and learn about each other but deny them participation for their issues on the world scene. This will result in repeated protracted struggles between governments and insurgencies worldwide.

It is also possible to change conditions quickly and have good outcomes. This could happen by limiting but not fully denying access between people. It would entail allowing issue groups to form if they are willing to collaborate with governments. This will allow issue groups to exist and to advance their issue but not grow or engage in insurgency. This may very well be a possible global counterinsurgency strategy.

There are long-term methods that can also have good outcomes. Granting wider access that helps embrace the participation of various issue organizations may also prove to be beneficial. However, it is possible to be victimized by groups that insist on violence. Nevertheless, this strategy is inclusive, empowering to the average human being, and does not hinder the development of world economy.

Current conditions are on the path to long-term bad outcomes. Unless something changes, this can go on indefinitely. There are ways to have good outcomes. This does not have to be all violence and no talking. Note that throughout this discussion taking the hard line on both sides yields the biggest costs. Political warfare rewards inclusion, and inclusion allows for the ownership of the issue in contention.

Are There Any Historical Parallels That Shed Light on What to Do?

Historical parallels that shed light on what to do are hard to find. Every war is different. Parallels can be problematic. We must be careful not to overgeneralize from what happened in the past to what might happen in the future. Still, historical parallels can be helpful in suggesting possible actions or warning of past mistakes. There are problems in finding a parallel. Insurgency without borders is new. Insurgency not aimed at liberating land or people from a national government is new. Also, finding a historical insurgency that is not part of some nation-state effort is difficult. If we use these problems as search criteria, many examples of insurgency must be left off the list.

One example does remain that sheds light on possibilities for global insurgencies. It is called King Philip's War, which was fought in southern New England in 1675 and 1676. On the surface, it looks like a straight war between colonists and native tribes. The reality is more complex. It was not a war of armies, fronts, and borders. The combatants lived with each other and knew each other. Instead, there were isolated enclaves of native camps and colonist cities, all within short travel distances between each other and among various forest landscapes. Each group was capable of mustering forces to fight, but these were not forces in being because they were costly and impractical to maintain constantly. Instead, these forces were called up as needed for a short time. That was the composition of both sides physically.

Politically, both sides were not simply defined. The English colonies in those days did not fully trust each other, particularly regarding borders. They would not fight each other, but they were not unified in all things.[24] The native tribes were also mixed. Some fought against the English, some were neutral or attempted to be neutral, and some sided with the English. Native tribes all had rivalries with each other.[25] Mistrust between the English and the native tribes arose over who had power and who had safety in the region. That mistrust brought the English to drive their allies away by lumping all the natives together and dealing with them out of fear for their own security.[26] That same mistrust led the natives to try to preserve what they saw as their dwindling power over their own future.

The natives wanting to fight were under the leadership of Philip, the son of Massasoit (who met the pilgrims in 1620), who led a series of raids on English colonies. They attacked Swansea, Rehoboth, and Taunton (in Massachusetts). A short time later, Philip's forces attacked Mendon, Brookfield, and Lancaster (also in Massachusetts). Other native tribes began to join Philip, and his movement grew stronger.[27] These raids were marked by surprise attack in which native warriors killed whoever they could, burned buildings, and left as quickly as they came. In those days, this was called the "native" way of war, and the natives (expert at hunting, tracking, and ambush) were well practiced at it.[28]

The English looked to the conventional warfare that they knew, forming armies, fighting battles, and engaging in sieges.[29] This was the Western way of war at that time. After 8 months, the English were visibly losing the conflict. Several colonist cities had been burned; some were not resettled for a decade after the end of the war.[30] Finally, the English relented on their decision to exclude native tribes from their side and met with Allied and Christian native groups to bring them into the war and to act with them. It was this decision that turned the tide of the war.

This war was marked on both sides by a scramble to find allies. Indeed, it became a war about popular support. Neither side was willing to allow anyone to be neutral. Rhode Island attempted to be neutral, and Providence was burned down by Philip's warriors.[31] The Narragansett tribe tried and wanted to be neutral, but English colonists would have none of it; they attacked them and drove them into the war on Philip's side.[32]

The English finally won this war. They did it by destroying support for Philip among the native tribes in the region. They changed to a strategy of growing their own support among the same tribes and, when raiding native tribes, granting amnesty to the warriors and executing their leaders. With this change in strategy, the English began pulling many of Philip's supporters into the English camp.[33] Finally, Philip was killed in the summer of 1676. Shortly after, his remaining supporters fell away, and the war ended.[34]

This was a war fought largely about issues; for the native tribes, the issues were about their future with the colonists and the power struggle they had with each other. For the English, it was about their insecurities over their own fragility and the degree of security they had living among the tribes. The side that was able to unite the most and divide their enemy the most won.

We can draw some general conclusions relevant today. This war was a bit about land on the English side, but it was much more about English insecurity regarding the numerous native tribes among whom they lived and insecurities among the native tribes over growing English colonies. Each native tribe was more of a nation than were the colonists. Yet, the native nations were transitory, picking up and moving to suit the seasons, forming armies only when the need arose. Warfare was waged across multiple areas using insurgency tactics of raid and ambush. Political issues drove both sides to seek popular support. The war was decided by who had inclusion and the best access to the largest number of people. These are the things needed to fight an insurgent war today.

Is This One of the Many Futures of War Proposed So Often?

This is one of the many futures of war proposed so often. After years of stagnation during which things did not change, change is now available. Many want to try to predict it. Global insurgency is not a revolution in military affairs. This is not about new weapons and communications. These things have their place, and they do affect the battlefield, but they are tools not ends in themselves. They gain attention because they are tangible and produce ponderous effects on the battlefield.

This future is about politics; it relies less on new battlefield tools. It relies more on results possible from violence. It is a future that postulates that a well-placed car bomb can do more than an aircraft carrier can to advance an agenda. People are still the major part of his mix. They add more nuance to war and require more of war. How was it possible for America to win all of its battles in Vietnam and lose the war? The answer stems from the idea that war goes beyond fighting battles. There really is no purely military point of view. That point of view only works if the other side also agrees to it. War is affected by politics in numerous ways, subtle and not, that must be taken into account to be successful.

This future of war proposes its return as an arm of politics. Because most recent wars (particularly those America has fought) have been total war for total victory, this has been forgotten. We are faced with its return now. We must become reacquainted with war in that way. We must become better using all of the tools to fight a war, not just the use of force, even though force is a powerful and important tool.

What Will This Future Look Like?

The future is foggy at best. Probably, no one should try to predict it. There are possibilities for both war and peace. The possibilities for war are as follows: (1) Contention exists between governments and peoples on a variety of issues; (2) popular groups compete with governments for support; (3) both sides decide if an issue is worth fighting over; (4) all people are faced with the possibility an issue elsewhere will bring violence to their homes; (5) all parties must make complex calculations of who they will include and will exclude; (6) the use of violence will more often be prepared before and after with political meaning and justification to the masses; (7) conflicts will arise suddenly and be internal as much as external to one nation or another.

The possibilities for peace are as follows: (1) better cooperation between governments and people; (2) worldwide support for salient issues; (3) the possibility of a world that works closer together; (4) the chance to see and intercept conflict before it gets out of hand. These possibilities will not stop war entirely. Some issues will always be nonnegotiable to some part of humanity. Which future is chosen depends on how the issues that arise are handled. If many issues are considered nonnegotiable, global insurgency could be a constant companion of humanity for a long time.

Implications

At the beginning of this book we observed that for a government or organization, fighting global insurgency hinges on the diverse portfolio. The economies of the world no longer respond to a generic one-size-fits-all approach, and it would seem warfare is going to go the same way. Changes in thought, in response, in preparation are in the offing for anyone who wishes to fight this kind of war. Many of those changes will be unpopular and resisted by those who are entrenched in the current system. But, the nature of warfare is that whoever wants to win it must change to meet its necessities. These changes will come in several forms.

First, it is necessary to steer away from the Gulf War as a response model to global insurgency warfare. It was a successful conventional war culminating trends in the conduct of conventional war dating to Napoleon. But, Napoleon also had problems with insurgency in Spain and Russia, two places in retrospect he should have left alone. Utilizing or fighting against unconventional warfare does not support the months of preparation that are needed for conventional forces to prepare to fight. Likewise, it is fruitless to apply generic war-fighting capabilities in a way that is not region specific.

What makes this type of warfare difficult is the need for off-battlefield action to win. In conventional wars, two forces meet on a battlefield. One wins; the other loses. The loser must try to fight again and win or risk losing the war. If an army is destroyed, the victorious army can dictate terms to a defenseless opponent. Conventional wars are predicated to battlefield action as the deciding factor in winning the war (but not in deciding precisely what was won). Contrast this with insurgency, for which losing on the battlefield is a loss on just one aspect of the overall war. Particularly for global insurgents, one can lose on a battlefield and still gain for the cause, as illustrated in chapters 1 and 3.

It is hard to fight if you do not know who is fighting. Global insurgencies will not be organized the way conventional forces are, and they will not make their organization and its participants explicit. It is necessary to know which issues are afoot because they draw organizations to the insurgency. Many people and organizations will join together to support an issue perceived to be in their common interest. Some participants may be a surprise to analysts in that they may not seem directly connected to the others. Finding this information out means engaging in mapping the components of an issue to see which other issues connect. Once the issues involved are known and understood, it will be possible to map out which factions attach to each issue and how they connect. It will be important to know which specific event or condition brings which organizations together. In this way, one can define the entity fought. The first step in fighting global insurgency is to know who the enemy is and why. Once you know this, you can figure out how to win.

Once the global insurgency is defined, defeating it calls in all forms of politics, not just defense. Not all factions in a global insurgency are geared to fighting. Some provide background support. It may be possible to fight some aspects of the insurgency while satisfying other participants so that they drop out. Only research can deduce which are which. It is possible that sanctions, treaties, or technology transfer will satisfy some organizations. This will bring other agencies and entities into the effort.

Whichever capability has the best answer to the need of the moment should be given the opportunity to act. This means, in a government or an organization, that any cabinet office or participating organization may have the lead on either side of a global insurgency at any moment. Other organizations on our side of the issue focus may also help. That is why it is important to map the issues and define the participants. Only then can a strategy be planned that can find out what the other side's factions want and either bring those factions to our side or isolate them as the case presents itself. It is also worth keeping in mind that these global insurgencies can be transitory as well as long-lived depending on how the issue group or constellation is composed and the stakes involved.

Physically destroying the global insurgency hinges on isolation and resource denial. They need connection for logistics and communications to arm, send/receive information, augment capabilities, and coordinate with others like any other force. The principle at work in combating insurgencies is to isolate and deny resources (money, supplies, etc.) to weaken identified cells. This can be done using both politics and force to isolate factions physically and politically and deny them support by coordination with other factions. Then, it is possible to destroy or co-opt isolated parts of the insurgency by force or siege. Even when successful, it is best to beware to keep victories sanitized. Declaring an area safe and moving on, rather than guarding what was won, guarantees a return of the enemy.

Caution should be observed against using the Libyan model against global insurgency. In that model, a nation is held responsible for terrorist actions and is punished accordingly. Little is heard from that nation afterward. It should be noted, however, that bombing Libya was not the end of America's terrorism problem, and overthrowing the Taliban probably will not be the end of its suicide bombing problems. States do sponsor terrorism, but in global insurgency, there is a difference between state and individual collaboration. That is, terrorists have been harbored and trained in a number of countries that abhor terrorism, including the United States. One cannot engage in Afghanistan-style operations in all of those countries without at some point being involved in a world war. Besides, other sources abound for collaboration with these insurgencies, including transnational criminal organizations, other nongovernmental organizations (NGOs), and personal fundraising.

It is almost a cliché to say that the world is greatly different now from the cold war. Many governments (less the Taliban) support the

United States to a lesser or greater degree in the wake of September 11, yet the vulnerability to global insurgency still exists. To defeat a global insurgency, many changes must occur. Rather than thinking of a monolithic entity that is the focus of our actions, it will be best to think instead in terms of issue supporters. If America is to lead the fight against terrorism worldwide, it will be necessary to consider how to help other governments track these insurgents and defend against them. Because global insurgency is the type of war these NGOs fight, defensive-oriented homeland security becomes an integral part of the successful prosecution of this war. America's ability to do it and export it will mean a great deal to our ultimate success or failure. If America and its allies cannot protect themselves from continued attack, their credibility will be lost while their enemies will grow bolder.

Currently, Al Qaeda and Iraqi insurgents are the focus of American efforts, but it is best to track those who oppose the overall U.S. agenda, oppose Israel, oppose antidrug agendas, or oppose world trade and be aware of how all of those issues may connect to each other to attract supporters. Because this is being called global insurgency, it should not be forgotten that it is interwoven into the fabric of everything, even in the United States. Global insurgency is not only a fight for armed forces but also a fight for all agencies and organizations with a stake in the outcome. That is the fundamental change in 21st century warfare, from the conventional to the insurgent, from the exclusive nation-on-nation power struggle to the inclusive grassroots movements of global insurgency.

Chapter 7

AL QAEDA AND HMS *DREADNOUGHT*

Al Qaeda represents a novel aspect of war in many ways, and in other ways they are not new at all. Setting Al Qaeda in context becomes important. It is the first global insurgency of any seriousness. It will not be the last; others will follow. They will have learned the lessons from Al Qaeda's failures and successes. They will execute better, much the same way all the battleships that were built after HMS *Dreadnought* were considerably better than HMS *Dreadnought* itself.

The actions of Al Qaeda in and of themselves are not new. What is new is the confluence of what they do, what they want, and why they are here now. Al Qaeda blends politics, action, and opportunity to make its existence. Similar occurrences to Al Qaeda have happened in the past. Some of those occurrences are even a direct ancestry. They do not shed much light on possible solutions to the Al Qaeda problem. They do, however, show that the ideas themselves are not new, and there are similar contexts in times past. If we can see why these things happened, it might help us understand better why global insurgency is happening now. One event, the Boxer Rebellion, shows how political context led to the rise of the rebellion. Another event, Nazi saboteurs coming to America, shows the context for choosing insurgency as an action rather than more conventional forms of attack.

The Boxer Rebellion occurred in China 100 years ago when Chinese peasants rose in rebellion against the Great Power dominance of China. This rebellion turned into a conflagration involving armies of all the great powers. But, beyond that, there are a number of nuances to the Boxer Rebellion that have relevance today. This was a conflict between an uncertain future and what it might be versus keeping life the same as times past. It was a conflict between tradition and modernity. It was a conflict over which was more important: economics or culture.

The Great Powers participating in the Boxer Rebellion were Great Britain, France, Russia, Germany, United States, Japan, Belgium, Italy, and Austria. Each nation (except the United States, which wanted open markets but not land) tried to stake out land in China for resources, markets, and spreading of the Christian religion. It must be remembered that this event happened during colonial times. Most of the powers sought land and economic concessions from the Chinese Imperial Court. These powerful nations brought their knowledge of improved technology and improved practices with them when they came to China. Although this was meant to be a boon facilitating Western economic practices, it also had adverse effects on the Chinese peasants. It made many traditional jobs obsolete and led to wide-scale unemployment.[1] It also brought about the perception that prosperity meant changing who they were and living the way the Great Powers lived.

The Chinese Imperial Court for its part wished that the world powers would leave China but did not have the power to force all of them to go. Although the Chinese army had numbers, its power was not enough to withstand any of the Great Powers individually, certainly not all of them together. The government running China was seen to be increasingly ineffective. It seemed to be continually giving concessions to the Great Powers for various things. They were looking for a way to remove the foreigners without provoking war.[2]

The Boxers seemed like the answer to the Imperial Court's desires. They were a supernatural cult that attracted a large following among Chinese peasants. They used spiritualism and the martial arts to preach that they were invincible and could drive out foreigners.[3] They had a great hatred of foreigners and Chinese converts to Christianity. This hatred brought them to attack rail and barge traffic and other economic symbols of the foreigners.[4] They formed an army to spread across China and destroy foreign influence.

These players came together with existing conditions in China to make the rebellion. The expansive foreign influence of the Great Powers changed China in many ways, very quickly. The population became disenchanted with the changes and what seemed like increasingly limited choices for their future. The Chinese Imperial Court seemed to be ineffective in meeting the peasants' concerns. This is what brought the violence of the Boxers to the surface. The Boxers began moving across China, attacking Christians and foreigners;

finally, they made their move to march on Beijing and destroy the Great Power legations situated there.

The Imperial Court saw the Boxers as an opportunity to finally rid China of Great Power influence and joined them, going as far as to issue an imperial edict exonerating the Boxers for all of the violence and placing the blame instead on Chinese Christians.[5] They hoped that finally the combined forces of the Boxers and Imperial Army would be enough to expel the Great Powers. The violence that came afterward was fearsome. In the end, the Imperial Court could not control the Boxers, who went on rampages in various places but could not be disciplined enough to defeat the Great Power forces. The Great Power legations in Beijing held out for 55 days against the Boxers while a Great Power coalition was formed among nations with legations in China and landed an expeditionary force in China that met both the Boxers and the Imperial Army and defeated them.

The Boxers were crushed, and Beijing was relieved. With the defeat of the Imperial forces, the last of the power of the Chinese Imperial Court was destroyed. The Great Powers then became firmly entrenched in China and would be until World War II, when Japan attempted to occupy the whole nation.

The results of the Boxer Rebellion are not the point here. Instead, consider these things. The Boxers rose because too much change happened too quickly in China for the peasants to be able to keep up with it and maintain any stability in their lives. Outside influences changed Chinese traditions and created discontent among the peasants. This resulted in outbreaks of violence, leading to the rise of the Boxers. The Boxers formed what amounted to a conventional army to fight against this, and they were crushed. It remains to be seen what might have happened if they formed an insurgency and fought that way. Mao subsequently did and, after decades of struggle, took power in China. It is easy to see that parallel conditions exist today around the world.

Al Qaeda attacks on America are not the first such attempts. In a precursor to global insurgency, the Nazis sent saboteurs to America during World War II. It is important to look at this to see the choices that the Nazis made and relate those choices to what is going on today. The Nazis recruited people who could live in the United States as Americans.[6] They were given training in sabotage and potential targets to destroy. These included targets such as aluminum processing plants, railways, bridges, water supplies, electrical systems, and hydro plants.[7] The saboteurs were furnished with false documents and false identities and sent to America to sabotage American industry and wreak havoc among the population.

Eight Nazis with money and explosives landed in America by submarine. A network of spies already existed in America to help them and collect intelligence on various targets.[8] In the event, the leader of one cell gave the operation up to the Federal Bureau of Investigation (FBI) within days of his arrival. The other seven were captured subsequently, and the plot was foiled. After that, with the heightened alert status of the FBI, the possibility of Nazi sabotage was less of a serious factor.

Here also, the results are less important for analysis than the choices made. The Nazis wanted to attack America but could not do it by air, sea, or land in large numbers. As a result, they chose insurgency as the means to attack the United States. They infiltrated the forces secretly. Contrast this with the Allied Normandy invasion, which utilized thousands of ships, and hundreds of thousands of men in a conventional invasion of Europe. The Nazis wanted to sabotage U.S. industry and economic strength and to kill people in railway stations and department stores, particularly in New York City.[9] The idea was to keep sending saboteurs to the United States until finally they had infiltrated what would amount to a large force in the United States to bring it down from within. This sort of insurgent action is what is chosen when someone decides that it is necessary to strike but there is no power to overwhelm. When conventional warfare is not an option, this sort of infiltration and sabotage always is. The parallels with Al Qaeda and its actions on September 11 are easy to see.

Changes in the world have brought us to this point. All changes come with good and bad results attached. There are some useful lessons to take away from this idea. Whenever great change happens quickly, there will be some negative reaction. Moving forward threatens the past and those who profit by that past. At the same time, standing still threatens the forward lookers and those who profit by potential. Overemphasizing either side could bring violent reaction.

Right now, global economics and information technology change life on Earth. Wealth generation is enhanced. The changes also install a system for prosperity, albeit one with boundaries. Those best able to use that system prosper from it. Those who cannot use it as well fall behind. The lesson of the Boxer Rebellion is that violent reactions can result from this.

For those who cannot use the system, it becomes the enemy. Violent reaction is directed against it and its chief proponents. Opponents of the system hope to defeat it or at least drive it off. Global economics and information technology actually placed the tools of war in people's hands (allowing them to fight the system) just as they place the tools of wealth in people's hands. This allows violent reactions from groups like Al Qaeda and others to be effective globally. It is easy to see Al Qaeda in everything that has been described so far in this chapter. We must see the properties of Al Qaeda to understand their actions and use that understanding as a window for future planning.

Al Qaeda Tested

In Chapter 6, we developed a template for visualizing global insurgency. It is a series of statements aimed at identifying its qualities and character. We can use that template as a test. The test will help solidify an understanding of Al Qaeda's characteristics. It will also solidify the worth of the template for analysis of future global insurgencies. Each statement will be examined in turn as to whether Al Qaeda fits the template or not. When it is completed, we should be able to see and understand a little bit better both global insurgency in general and Al Qaeda as a global insurgent movement.

The insurgency generates services like governments to fight wars. Al Qaeda has a funding apparatus that feeds its operations. It procures weapons.[10] It forms plans. It collects intelligence.[11] It crafts a message to gather support. It engages in formal training of its operatives, ranging from fundamentalist indoctrination, to reconnaissance, to suicide attack.[12] Al Qaeda not only operates with authority over its cells, but also operates in mutual agreement with other groups. Apparently, there is room for other groups to either join Al Qaeda and take orders or collaborate with them somewhat autonomously.

The movement seeks popular support. No Middle Eastern governments are talking seriously about liberating the lands of the Middle East or freeing them from the influence of global economics. Al Qaeda, rather than attempt to take over a single nation, is instead appealing to people in all nations to join them. They have not attempted to form a conventional army. Instead, they recruit regular people who are highly motivated to serve the cause. They claim they were provoked to act by U.S. actions in the Gulf War and expand their reach and their effectiveness by cooperating with the like-minded worldwide to act with them or on their behalf.

Global insurgencies are composed of diverse groups in multiple locations. Al Qaeda is not monolithic or homogeneous. It has cells in over 70 countries, including the United States.[13] It also has ties to groups in Iraq, to HAMAS in Palestine, to the Harakat organizations in Pakistan, and to Chechen guerrillas, among many other groups, including criminal organizations around the world.[14]

The insurgency is connected and motivated by an issue. Al Qaeda uses a need to defend Islam as a powerful motivator for action. Osama bin Laden calls for anyone who truly believes to kill Americans whenever and wherever possible.[15] The issue paints existing governments as ineffective or collaborators with the West. The insurgents avow they cannot live with the current situation as it stands. Another feature of the ideology is that jihad must take place everywhere until all submit.[16] This both calls and involves people all over the world in the insurgency. Indeed, some in the movement believe that no Muslim is blameless until the goals of the movement are achieved.[17] With this philosophy, they seek to attract and recruit all Muslims in all nations to their cause.

The issue attracts many groups with related sympathetic concerns. The central issue for Al Qaeda is an attack on Islam illustrated by the presence in Saudi Arabia of Western powers led by the United States. They have been successful in getting other groups to agree with that if not with Al Qaeda's leadership. The list of affiliates grows and changes often.[18] Even those who disagree with violence do not seem to oppose that sentiment. Al Qaeda of courses vilifies any who do not agree with their stance. This tactic buys Al Qaeda the time to convince the unsure to join them. This is not just happening in Saudi Arabia. It is happening from Morocco, to the Philippines, to the Western Hemisphere, perhaps anywhere Muslim communities exist. However, one should not take that to mean that all Muslims or even all fundamentalists support Al Qaeda. It simply means that Al Qaeda looks at all communities as opportunities to gain support and followers.

The attractiveness of the issue feeds the connections that make for global power. Al Qaeda rails against the effects of global economics. Its issues are anti-Semitic and anti-Christian as well as anti-Western. Al Qaeda tries to bridge between concerns attempting, in some cases succeeding, to bring together both Shi'ite and Sunni communities to work together.[19] Al Qaeda tries to gather all those whose cause fits in some way with their cause. Some of these groups may not care about the U.S. presence in the Middle East but hate the influence of global economics on their lives and hold America responsible. These groups will act with Al Qaeda, just like others who might do so for religious reasons.

The insurgency can coordinate action in multiple places. Al Qaeda can project power worldwide. They can link from nation to nation for any action they care to take. The United States, incidentally, does the same thing when it projects power abroad. Only a handful of nations in modern times have ever been defined as having a power projection capability. These nations generally have aircraft carriers, large fleets, and intercontinental-range aircraft, and they are nations we know well: the United States, Russia, Britain, France, and China. Now, however, Al Qaeda also can project power globally. From September 11, we can note that the connections to make that attack happen ran from Afghanistan, to Germany, to Boston and New York. Bombing the USS *Cole* probably required coast watchers all over the Mediterranean Sea, agents in regional governments, and of course the bombers in Yemen. In this way, Al Qaeda destroyed the old paradigm of power projection and replaced it with a new paradigm in which power projection is less about physical infrastructure and platforms and more about people and what they are willing to do locally on behalf of global insurgency.

The insurgency can take actions in multiple places. Al Qaeda has attacked in the United States, Yemen, Kenya, Indonesia, Madrid, the Philippines, Britain, and Iraq. They have affiliates in Palestine territory, in Indonesia, and in the Philippines with the Moros and Abu Sayyaf. They give license to any who wish to act on behalf of Al Qaeda and applaud the actions of any who take up their cause. This widens Al Qaeda's ability to cover the world and take action anywhere. This allows Al Qaeda to claim a global strike capability, which most nations on earth do not possess.

The actions of the insurgents connect directly to the issue cause. Al Qaeda leadership noted how catastrophe has repeatedly led Western forces to leave the areas where they were engaging in operations in the past. It was because the losses Western powers suffered outweighed potential short-term gains. Al Qaeda also tries to make the cost of staying in a place too high. Actions like the attacks on September 11 also demonstrate Al Qaeda can hurt the United States when most of the governments of this planet cannot. It should also be noted that the targets associated with that attack were targets associated with globalism and American power. Likewise, because the issue at hand deals with the Middle East, it tends to explain why there have been no wide-scale campaigns of attacks in United States because the issue is a "liberation" of the Middle East; because the people who are recruited are people who generally live in the Middle East, the actions taking place tend to serve and center around that.

The insurgency uses all tools to advance the issue and grow its power. Al Qaeda has had a string of successful actions that increased the strength of the issue until it has become one of, if not the, top threat to security on the planet. All governments must wonder now if Al Qaeda is subverting their authority or getting ready to attack them. Each success is a recruiting tool with great propaganda strength and is portrayed as a milestone to the ultimate goal. Each success shows the weakness of Al Qaeda's opponents. From Afghanistan, to Yemen, to Africa, they are recruiting people, not radiating out from one place to those places. Al Qaeda is simply adding them on. Because it is a religious issue, it is important everywhere the religion exists.

The issue and the insurgency exhibit global influence. Al Qaeda has supporters in over 70 countries. Each day brings the possibility of more. In many nations, frustration, unemployment, and poverty prevail. Warfare is being brought to meet the context they set. Politics is being brought to deal with the Al Qaeda agenda. Al Qaeda can reward joiners with money or status and can punish any opponent they choose, as already shown.

The issue expands and contracts with each interaction. Al Qaeda has been dealt setbacks after each attack. It regenerates each time and will continue to do so as long as Al Qaeda issues are salient. As the salience goes, so goes the resilience. For example, communism is no longer a salient issue and has trouble gathering support from people. Al Qaeda exhibits the characteristics of global insurgency. This implies that defeating Al Qaeda will be about solving, discrediting, or assimilating their agenda. The issues Al Qaeda champions have been around for years. They were not considered salient in the cold war. The superpowers were largely uninterested in dealing with those issues, and the governments of the Middle East were largely unsuccessful in dealing with them. Now, those issues are salient to people all over the Middle East. Because of the religious aspect Al Qaeda is trying to emphasize, the issue becomes even more powerful.

The importance of Al Qaeda as a phenomenon can be seen in its effects. It has pulled political agendas of the world in unplanned direction. It has pulled modern warfare similarly in unplanned directions. There are grave implications for both of these events. We must look at them more closely to understand their impact.

Unplanned Political Agendas

Governments in the past used intelligence to discover the agendas of other governments. This was how governments discovered potential opponents. They then oriented their own agenda to meet that threat. They would also orient their war-fighting capability the same way. This is how traditional security planning has been done for quite some time.

In light of this, there are good reasons why some believed that Francis Fukuyama was right when he said we have reached an end of history. When communism fell, there seemed to be agreement on the benefits of capitalism and free markets. It seemed like the pursuit of free markets and open political systems would be the norm for most of the world, if not all of it. It seemed like there was more agreement than disagreement among governments about the future of the world.

Not long after communism's fall, violence erupted among ethnic subgroups around the world. Violence occurred in Bosnia, Kashmir, and Rwanda, among many other places. Ethnic groups began fighting either for the opportunity to decide their own future or out of fear that they would not be able to decide their own future. When communism fell, for many it brought with it the possibility of power and freedom after years under the old system.

For some time, the governments of the world tried to ignore these events. Sometimes, they would try to negotiate agreements. Sometimes, they would try to extinguish it with bombing or cruise missiles. Sometimes, they treated it as a law enforcement problem. It seemed like they never really dealt with the underlying issues. These methods might have worked against isolated incidents, but they were going to fail against a worldwide insurgency campaign like the one Al Qaeda has been waging. Insurgents like Al Qaeda neither deter nor compromise. Talking, threatening, even chastising have little effect on them.

Al Qaeda has become a prominent part of the world security landscape as a result of September 11. It is a security concern now for most nations. Because it uses infiltration and hopes to recruit followers in many nations, it also becomes a domestic concern in many nations. This makes Al Qaeda a political entity with an agenda that must be countered. Every nation on earth must spend at least some time factoring Al Qaeda into their future plans. This has the effect of changing the agendas of most governments. Usually, only powerful nations are capable of this. If Al Qaeda is allowed to grow larger, it can become more powerful and harder to defend against.

Al Qaeda's rise is similar to the rise of Nazism leading to World War II. What is similar are the conditions in Europe that lead to the rise, Nazi ideology, and the support the Nazis were able to get. The Nazis started as a minority party. They were never supposed to rule Germany. At the beginning, few took them seriously. This was in spite of the fact that Hitler warned the world of his intentions his book *Mein Kampf*.

Certain conditions in Germany prevailed that allowed the Nazis to rise. Weimar Germany was the defeated remnant of imperial Germany. It was made to be weak and stay weak as the victorious powers of World War I wanted to ensure that Germany would be powerless by virtue of the Versailles Treaty. There was widespread unemployment.

When the Depression hit, Germany's economy was in shambles. This left the people of a once-powerful and prosperous Germany very discontented with their lives and their possible future. The Weimar government seemed to be ineffective in fixing these problems. The future for both the nation and for individual Germans seemed bleak.

The conditions were ripe for the German people to follow anyone who seemed might be effective in fixing their problems. The Nazis asserted an ideology that seemed to answer the questions of many in Germany and pose solutions to their problems. Nazi ideology said the German race is and should be master of the world, and all other races must submit to it.[20] Furthermore, the Nazis asserted that subjugation by a master race was better for subject peoples than freedom.[21] This includes not just Germany, but anywhere Germans live.[22] Indeed, the Nazis asserted the right to force these principles on all Germans.[23] Germany's problems, according to the Nazis, stemmed from other races, all of whom must be subjugated or destroyed (which they defined as an act of self-preservation), and of course from the inability of the present government to deal with these problems.[24] The Nazis painted anyone who disagreed with them as an enemy and traitor, and they were uncompromising on the possibility that anyone else could be right.[25]

The rise of the Nazis was slow at first while recruiting and political maneuvering took place. The Nazis offered an appealing path to follow for the discontented, particularly war veterans. They promised to fix the problems of the nation and restore German power. They also promised to repudiate the Versailles Treaty provisions that weakened Germany.[26] Each year, the Weimar government seemed less and less effective, and more and more people became willing to support the Nazis or at least tolerate them.[27]

Finally, the Nazis gained enough electoral support to form a new German government. They immediately replaced government officials with Nazis.[28] Following that, they outlawed other parties and any form of dissent.[29] This was all accepted because they began to have successes on the world stage; with each success, they gained more support within Germany and in other countries. This allowed the Nazis to redefine German nationalism their own way. This redefinition made individual Germans have to choose to serve the Nazis and be considered a good German or oppose the Nazis and be considered a bad German. This was true both inside Germany and worldwide.

The rise of the Nazis to power changed the landscape and calculations of the world. Germany was not supposed to be powerful again. With the rise of the Nazis, Germany became not only powerful, but also hostile and had their eyes on expanding to any nation with a German minority. The other nations had to adapt their future plans accordingly whether they wanted to or not. This brought nations to choose sides internationally and brought about domestic questions of Nazi infiltration by "fifth columnists."

The rise of the Nazis has implications that track with the rise of Al Qaeda. The Nazis started small and unknown. No one took them seriously. They were able to grow support against ineffective or indifferent opposition. It should be noted that Lenin and Mao accomplished similar rises to power in Russia and China, respectively. Al Qaeda started small and was not supposed to be very important. Key features of the Nazis relevant to Al Qaeda include the following: There was an ideology that answered questions and seemed to solve people's problems; people were willing at least to listen; no hard opposition existed to the Nazis; the people were willing to follow success.

Al Qaeda has similarities to the Nazi paradigm worth noting. They look to discontented people for support. They sought those who fear their future and where it might lead. They provide an ideology that points out who the enemy is, explains why things are the way they are, and tells them all what must be done to fix them. They make Muslim governments seem either ineffective or collaborators with the authors of all the problems. Al Qaeda seems to be growing steadily at the very least. They have survived more than 3 years of war with the United States, something neither the Nazis nor imperial Japan was able to do. They hope to force Muslims to choose them. If Al Qaeda becomes powerful enough, they, like the Nazis, could decide what being a Muslim means. The world might then have to face a mass of discontented people following a hostile ideology. This could make for a long and bloody conflict. Al Qaeda has already changed the political landscape greatly. How much more will change if they are allowed to grow?

A New Path for Warfare

Warfare has also been changed by Al Qaeda's global insurgency. This implies that warfare was supposed to look some other way, and it was. It was supposed to be more conventional. That was because it was taken for granted that the important issues would be championed by nations and decided by national armed forces.

The cold war was the paradigm for warfare the world lived with for decades. The issue was whether communism or capitalism would dominate the world. Warfare was centered on battle between tank armies, air wings, and large naval fleets. This was supposed to take place in the shadow of large numbers of nuclear weapons. This type of warfare featured a competition of arms technology and large numbers of weapons. But, the cold war failed to turn hot. Communism crumbled, and a new paradigm was sought.

The Gulf War in Iraq occurred in 1990 and brought about what seemed to be the new conventional warfare model with it. The Gulf War seemed to herald a victory of technology and training over numbers. Power projection and precision-guided weaponry seemed to be the hallmark of power in the post-Communist era. The preeminence of the United States seemed firmly established by this war. War was still a conventional conflict. The Allied and Iraqi armed forces fought until one side was defeated. After this, the politicians came together to decide what meaning to assign to the fighting.

After the Gulf War, high-tech weapons and power projection combined to form what seemed to be the new model of war. Other nations try to mimic the United States as their finances allow. The United States decided to put their preeminence to work using power projection into regional trouble spots. By this, the United States would use power projection as a tool for enforcing stability around the world. The main challenge was seen as rogue states or would-be breakaway states or possibly future rivals for U.S. power.[30]

This evolution of conventional conflicts projected a future emphasized by conventional warfare. Here, the focus was to be on finding potential U.S. power rivals or regional dictators to fight. The problems to be solved in this new conventional warfare model would include how best to combine forces and how best to use new advances in weapons and communications technology. The projected future was a more efficient, technically sophisticated conventional war. The better a nation was at this, it was felt, the further ahead that nation would pull away from nations that could not use this type of warfare as well.

Another evolution was going on at the same time. This was an evolution of insurgency conflict. This evolution hinted at pulling warfare to the unconventional side. We saw an indication of the problems insurgency would create for conventional forces in Vietnam. Really, this effectiveness goes back to World War I. The effectiveness of insurgency was dismissed out of the idea that one can survive using insurgency, but one cannot win with it. Forces designed for conventional warfare have always had a problem with insurgency. The effectiveness of insurgency, however, was hidden by the awe-inspiring power of the conventional forces used in the cold war and the first Gulf War.

Beyond Vietnam, the Soviet Afghan war was another indicator of this parallel evolution. Soviet forces invading Afghanistan were trained for conventional war in Europe.[31] They were not configured to fight against small insurgent units.[32] They were not configured to fight as small units themselves.[33] They did not have the resources to tend to their own security and carry on an offensive.[34] The Mujahedin for their part were able to deny the Soviets free movement and new recruits with their operations by virtue of their insurgent strategy and the political support they were able to generate.[35] Ultimately, with the help of Muslim nations and the United States, the insurgents made it too costly for the Soviets to stay in Afghanistan, and they left.

The American-led peacekeeping mission to Somalia is another step in the evolution of insurgency. Peacekeeping turned to hostilities in Mogadishu, the capital of Somalia. Because it was peacekeeping, limits were placed on the usage of tanks and air power for taking action. That meant that infantry combat would be emphasized inside the city. This denied the United States much of what had been its combat advantages in long-range precision-guided weaponry. This restraint was unavoidable because of the politics of peacekeeping and the proximity of the noncombatant population to the fighting. The results were firefights in which casualties happened on both sides. Once more, it was judged that the costs of pulling out were less than the costs of staying in Somalia.

Chechnya also offers an example of the rising effectiveness of insurgency. Chechen insurgents did their fighting at close range in cities. This made the armor and air power of the Russians less useful.[36] Russian forces were not built for insurgency warfare in cities. They had communication and interoperability problems.[37] They were driven out of the city of Grozny by the insurgents. The Russians returned, but as this book was being written they still have not defeated the Chechens, although much of the area is in shambles.

There are undeniable implications springing from this parallel rise of insurgency warfare alongside conventional warfare. The implications show that warfare has been pulled away from the conventional model. Since the first Gulf War, there has been little nation-on-nation fighting. Warfare has migrated to cities, where insurgents hide and fight, and until recently conventional wisdom warned armies to bypass.[38] Warfare is no longer just a contest of professional armies. Direct popular support of any side has become a decisive part of victory. The United States and its allies are spread thin in contesting global insurgency.

Warfare has become more of a strategic concern as insurgency takes advantage of context instead of battlefield power. Fighting in cities dilutes the effectiveness of modern weapons. Fighting in cities disguises insurgents, enhancing surprise. Insurgent warfare mixes politics directly with violence, affecting its context. Insurgent warfare is waged to enhance costs and consume enemy resources, raising the cost of victory to the other side.

Making popular support a direct necessity tips the advantage away from conventional conflict. Insurgents live by popular support. They use it for recruiting, for intelligence, for gathering money, and for weapons. Insurgency directly involves the masses in the struggle, whether it is active or passive. By contrast, conventional forces sequester themselves from people. They live in camps, and they fight as a self-contained entity. The popular support aspect of insurgency means a win by force of arms alone is unlikely.

In short, the effectiveness of traditional conventional warfare has been diluted somewhat. Politics has moved away from nation-versus-nation disputes settled by arms. Fighting has moved away from battlefields and into cities. It matters less how powerful conventional forces are if no one is willing to fight conventional wars. This means that conventional forces must change the way they fight to be effective.

Al Qaeda has become the culmination of those effects. They are only the first. Others will come after and will be better. Here is what Al Qaeda has changed about the world. Without benefit of a nation to call their own, they strike worldwide, having already struck in New York, Washington, Madrid, and Aden, among many other places. They use surprise rather than open attack. By extension, they do not present a solid target for opponents. Conventional methods used against them seem to have fewer long-term effects. The navies of the United States and the world have been all but taken out of the picture as weapons against insurgency. Homeland security is now a multibillion-dollar concern in the United States. Questions are being raised about the effectiveness of the U.S. multibillion-dollar intelligence apparatus. Our emphasis has changed from war with tanks to war with infantry.

Al Qaeda has changed what the future of warfare will be in spite of the desires of many professionals worldwide. This is because plotting such a future is incomplete without enemy interaction. We did not choose this enemy. Al Qaeda and others are carrying war where it wants to go. Conventional warfare is done by agreement. That is, mirror image forces fight each other in formal battles to decide an issue. Insurgency warfare is made by disagreement. That is, they attempt to change the conditions and contexts under which the war will be fought in ways that favor them. To defeat Al Qaeda and future insurgencies, we must answer their attempts at changing the conditions and context of conflict. If they have surprise and initiative on their side, they get to choose when and how war will be fought. This also is war by disagreement. To win, we must retake surprise and initiative and force insurgents to fight outside their favored contexts and conditions.

What Can We Do?

To fight this type of war, some things must change. The changes are more about thoughts, perceptions, and how governments solve problems rather than anything physical. The first change is that governments must learn to see the issues that are transnational and could become violent. We know that religion is one such issue. There may be others, such as the environment, labor, and wealth distribution. These are the new potential threats, and governments must analyze them as well as threats from other governments.

Governments must learn to assimilate the issues, and the agents, of the opposition into their own camp. The issue will be the key to winning politically. If governments are going to defeat global insurgents, they must learn to take control of the issue politically and attract support from as many quarters as possible for their side of the issue. A failure here loses a government its legitimacy and prolongs the conflict.

Governments must learn to see and react to situations quicker. Intelligence that helps governments see potential threats and outcomes will give governments a longer lead time to be ready for emerging threats. It will allow governments and their armed forces to react quicker to events. Insurgents move quickly. Governments also must learn to do so if they are to prevail.

Strategic planners must move from countering nations to a counterinsurgency orientation. They must plan on counterinsurgency as a feature of their overall security planning, not as an afterthought to it. Trying to pick the new "enemy" nation is overly simplistic and does not take into account the insurgencies that have risen or will rise. No government can invade and occupy all of the nations it identifies as troublesome, particularly against an insurgency spread out over multiple nations. Governments must still be ready to take on other nations because that threat will not just disappear, but insurgencies are more virulent and spread more easily if left unchecked. More emphasis must be placed on combating insurgencies. It used to be that America planned to fight conflicts in multiple regions, and that was a difficult proposition. Currently, planning to fight one insurgency is proving difficult for America. How much more difficult will it be to plan and fight against two global insurgencies?

Governments must learn to reconnect violence with political goals. They must make use of force directly connected to politics and demonstrate that connection to the people they are trying to influence. They cannot wait for the fighting to be over to make such connections as in conventional conflict. The insurgents do not wait to make those connections, and they make a point of trying to influence the masses with every act. Governments that do not do the same thing will fall behind in attracting people to their cause, and this will postpone any thoughts of victory they might have.

Governments must fix the imbalance that exists between wealth production and security. Everyone must be made to understand the push and pull between wealth production and security and how emphasizing one comes at a cost to the other. Wealth production works best when security does not impede it. Good security slows the speed of transactions that help produce wealth. In the 1980s, cold war security was emphasized, and most of the world market was not accessible to Western entrepreneurs. In the 1990s, that changed, and barriers were broken down to expand the production of wealth. Seesawing back and forth between the two is not a good idea. Governments and their people must learn to live with a certain level of wealth production that is less than the open fire hose of the 1990s and a level of security that is good but not walls and a moat. The American government in particular needs both wealth and security to maintain its "hard" and "soft" power to successfully fight global insurgency.

Governments must learn to stop advocating popular disinvolvement. Governments need popular support but often settle for popular acquiescence for their policies. This is no revelation, and it has worked in a number of governments throughout time, but to fight a war in which issue politics is a key to victory, this must change. People must be mobilized to act to advance the issue and the government agenda. This has not happened for the "war on terror," particularly in the field of homeland security. People must be activated and energized to shoulder the burdens of this war like any other. That popular mobilization is another key part of the winning strategy of war against insurgency.

Governments must learn to multitask and reconfigure quicker and easier because there may be more than one insurgency to handle at a time. They must find ways to be ready to fit any situation and be what that situation requires. This is no longer a one-size-fits-all world, not economically and not politically. Governments must take each situation that arises as it is and configure their agendas, armed forces, intelligence, funding, training, and procurement to the situation. Insurgents do it. Governments must do it also, learning to be flexible and not doctrinaire in their choices and actions. This probably sounds vague, and it is. Being what the situation requires is vague until we know what the situation is. Once we know the situation, we need to be able to identify what the situation requires and do it rather than what we "do best" or "know how to do" if it is not relevant.

Reforming intelligence is good, but reforming homeland security is better. In an insurgency, surprise attack against weak points is standard operating procedure. This means nonmilitary targets are attacked, usually in public places. People feel the effects of these attacks more keenly than the military will. Such actions affect popular support for governments and issues.

Failure of security against insurgency can be catastrophic, as we all saw on September 11, 2001. It cannot be sustained often without the loss of popular support and governmental authority. Four years later, homeland security (the safeguard against these attacks) has not exhibited uniform effectiveness. This is not the forum to bash homeland security, but it clearly is not ready to defend America from insurgency, and it must be. If America cannot be defended, its credibility will suffer.

The fact that nothing has happened in America since September 11 is not necessarily a sign of readiness. Al Qaeda operates worldwide, and it has been active elsewhere. But for them, the point is not affecting America so much as gaining Muslim support for their agenda. That they have not hit America again is probably as much about the way they service their agenda as it is about American homeland security. The U.S. government needs to activate people and equip them to think and act for their own safety. It is obvious to any observer that has not happened yet. America remains vulnerable to insurgencies no matter where American forces are sent. A successful attack on America can damage any efforts the government wishes to make abroad. That must be fixed. As Sun Tzu once said: "The good fighters of old first put themselves beyond the possibility of defeat, and then waited for the opportunity of defeating the enemy."[39]

For governments in general, but for America in particular, some things should stay the same. We should maintain our unmatched ability to wage war. We should also maintain our unmatched ability to generate wealth. We must keep our ability to project power worldwide. The possibility of conventional war still exists, and we must stay able to wage it. Yet, we must change enough to be able to wage counterinsurgency warfare in a number and variety of places. We must not forget our soft power influence on the world. If politics is now an important component of winning, then our ability to convince people to follow us is of paramount importance. In other words, we must keep what makes us powerful but change its usage and its emphasis. We have the power to win this way. That said, we must make our thinking as useful as our firepower and watch issues for threats as much as we watch governments.

It will be both hard and easy to adapt. The rules and conventions for making wealth and war are part of what make America powerful. People in power in many nations rely on those rules to keep their power. Yet, some of America's opponents will go outside the rules and make it so that some conventions need revision or change. Not all of those in power are interested in helping change; in fact, they will be obstacles to change. On the other hand, some who want too much to change will make wrong changes just to be able to change. If there is a rush to change without clear thinking, it may move us in the wrong direction. The reaction of our opponents will decide the value of our change. We must adapt when we do not have the initiative and innovate when we do. Not every good idea can be practically applied.

We do have advantages in adapting to these concerns. Our heterogeneity should make adapting easier. We can have a variety of people, knowledge, and points of view, and that gives us a catalog of ideas like no other nation on earth. We have a spirit of entrepreneurship that constantly moves us forward and delivers us better possibilities for the future. Our diversity can give us an affinity for many cultures and issues if we let it. Our ideas, our entrepreneurship, and our diversity are all tools useful in peace or war to achieve our goals.

There is no reason for the United States not to do better at fighting global insurgency. The question is, will our own entrenched interests allow it? The answer hinges on whether people believe we can lose this kind of war. We can choose not to adapt and use old thinking and methods to combat insurgency, but there will be consequences. We can hold nations responsible for the insurgencies, rightly or not. But, the issues fostering insurgency and their related violence will continue to crop up in increasing number and combination. Casualties will increase and be harder to justify, and the violence will happen at home as well as abroad.

These conflicts could go on and on. Human and material costs can rise beyond an easy ability to forecast. Most commitments of force abroad will be for the long term. The more we exclude people from a solution, the more our enemies will include them if they can.

Adapting could bring just as many casualties as not adapting but perhaps with less sense of futility attached if it seems like progress is being made. We can become like a dinosaur stuck in the tar pit... powerful, but unable to move or save ourselves. It is a dire warning but only of what may be, not what must be. The choice is all of ours to make.

Notes

Chapter 1: The Case for Global Insurgency

1. Clausewitz, *On War*, edited and translated by Michael Howard and Peter Paret, Princeton, Princeton University Press, 1976, p. 87.

2. Mao Tze Tung, *On Guerrilla Warfare*, translated by Brigadier General Samuel B. Griffith, USMC (ret) (New York: Praeger Publishers, 1967), p. 50.

3. Stanley Karnow, *Vietnam: A History* (Middlesex, U.K.: Penguin Books, Ltd., 1983), p. 536.

4. Ibid., p. 525.

Chapter 2: Leadership and Mobilization

1. David Ronfeldt, John Arquilla, Graham E. Fuller, and Melissa Fuller, *The Zapatista Social Netwar in Mexico* (Santa Barbara, CA: RAND, 1998), p. 1.

2. Ibid.

3. Ibid., p. 37.

4. Ibid., p. 50.

5. Ibid., p. 51.

6. Ibid.

7. Ibid., p. 70.

8. Ibid., pp. 58–60.

9. Ibid., p. 140.

10. Phil Williams, "Transnational Criminal Organizations: Strategic Alliances," *The Washington Quarterly*, CSIS/MIT, Winter 1995: 62.

11. Ibid.

12. Ibid., p. 64.

13. Ibid., p. 65.

14. Ibid., pp. 66–67.

15. Ibid., p. 68.

16. Greg Lefevre, Katharine Barrett, and Associated Press, "Seattle Mayor Declares Civil Emergency as WTO Unrest Grows," CNN, 11/30/99; date accessed 11/13/01, www.cnn.com/us/9911/30/wto.03/index.html.

17. Ibid.

18. Don Knapp and Associated Press, "Activists to WTO: Put People Over Profits," CNN, 11/29/99; 11/13/01, www.cnn.com/US/9911/29/wto.seattle.02index.html.

19. CNN, "Purported bin Laden Tape Endorses Zarqawi," CNN, 12/27/04; 01/12/05, www.cnn.com/2004/WORLD/meast/12/27/binladen.tape/index.html.

20. Associated Press, "Concern Over Radical Relief Group," CNN, 01/06/05; 01/12/05, www.cnn.com/2005/WORLD/asiapcf/01/06/aceh.radicals/ap/index.html.

21. United Nations, DPINGO Section, www.un.org/dpi/ngosection/asp/form.asp, 8/28/03.

22. Mike Dolan, "The Indirect Action Network," pp. 228–29, in Mike Prokosch and Laura Raymonds, eds., *The Global Activists Manual* (New York: Thunder's Mouth Press/Nation Books, 2002), p. 229.

23. Martin Stephan, "The Fight Against Boise Cascade," pp. 26–31, in Mike Prokosch and Laura Raymonds, eds., *The Global Activists Manual* (New York: Thunder's Mouth Press/Nation Books, 2002), p. 27.

24. Starhawk, "How We Really Shut Down the WTO," pp. 134–39, in Mike Prokosch and Laura Raymonds, eds., *The Global Activists Manual* (New York: Thunder's Mouth Press/Nation Books, 2002), pp. 134–35.

25. Maria Garrido and Alexander Halavais, "Mapping Networks of Support for the Zapatista Movement," in Martha McCaughey and Michael D. Ayers, eds., *Cyberactivism in Theory and Practice* (New York: Routledge, 2003), p. 169.

26. Starhawk, p. 135.

27. Mary Beth Maxwell, "Coalition Building: Lessons From the Jobs With Justice Model," pp. 72–77, in Mike Prokosch and Laura Raymonds, eds., *The Global Activists Manual* (New York: Thunder's Mouth Press/Nation Books, 2002), p. 73.

28. Andrew Boyd, "Billionaires Crash the Extreme Costume Ball," pp. 152–60, in Mike Prokosch and Laura Raymonds, eds., *The Global Activists Manual* (New York: Thunder's Mouth Press/Nation Books, 2002), p. 158.

29. Howard Rheingold, *Smartmobs: The Next Social Revolution* (Cambridge, MA: Perseus Publishing, 2003), pp. 157–58.

30. Boyd, p. 159.

Chapter 3: Global Insurgency Warfare

1. Robert B. Asprey, *War in the Shadows: The Guerrilla in History*, Vol. 1 (New York: Doubleday and Co., 1974), p. 477.

2. David Schoenbrun, *Soldiers of the Night: The Story of the French Resistance* (New York: Meridian, 1980), p. 357.

3. Asprey, p. 478.

4. Schoenbrun, p. 372.

5. Ibid., p. 373.

6. David Ronfeldt, John Arquilla, Graham E. Fuller, and Melissa Fuller, *The Zapatista Social Netwar in Mexico* (Santa Barbara, CA: RAND, 1998), p. 47.

7. Timothy L. Thomas, "The Battle for Grozny: Deadly Classroom for Urban Combat," *Parameters* (Summer 1999), 96.

8. U.S. Department of State, "Patterns of Global Terrorism, Appendix B: Background Information on Designated Foreign Terrorist Organizations," 04/30/03; 08/28/03, http://www.state.gov/s/ct/rls/pgtrpt/2002/html/1999/pf.htm.

9. John M. Collins, *Military Geography For Professionals and the Public* (Washington, DC: Brasseys, 1998), p. 198.

Chapter 4: Intelligence

1. Central Intelligence Agency, CIA Factbook on Intelligence 2002: The Intelligence Cycle, date accessed 12/10/03, www.odci.gov/cia/publications/factell/intelligence_cycle.html.

2. Central Intelligence Agency, CIA Today–Different Kinds of Intelligence, 12/21/03, www.odci.gov/cia/publication/cia_today/ciatoday_06.shtml.

3. CIA, CIA Today.

4. Barbara Grewe, Michael Jacobson, Thomas Eldridge, and Susan Ginsberg, "Staff Statement No. 10—Threats and Responses in 2001," in Steven Strasser, ed., *The 9/11 Investigations* (New York: Public Affairs Reports, 2004), p. 285.

5. Dorothy E. Denning, *Information Warfare and Security* (Reading, MA: Addison Wesley Longman, Inc., 1999), p. 80.

6. Fuld Gilad Herring Academy of Competitive Intelligence, 1/20/04, www.academyci.com/about.

7. Dan Verton, *Black Ice: The Invisible Threat of Cyberterrorism* (Emeryville, CA: McGraw Hill, 2003), p. 126.

8. Denning, p. 177.

9. CIA, CIA Today.

10. David P. Dilegge and Mathew Van Konynenberg, "The Chechens and Urban Operations: View From the Wolves Den," pp. 171–84, in *Non-state Threats and Future Wars* (London: Frank Cass and Co., Ltd, 2003), p. 183.

11. Ibid., p. 183.

12. Kevin Mitnick and William L. Simon, *The Art of Deception* (Indianapolis, IN: Wiley Publishing, 2002).

13. Aero Bureau Corp., "News From Above," 1/20/04, www.Aerobureau.com.

14. Space Imaging, 1/20/04, www.spaceimaging.com/corporate/default.htm.

15. ImageSat International, About Us, 1/20/04, www.imagesatintl.com/aboutus/aboutus.shtml.

16. Ibid., Infrastructure, 1/20/04, www.imagesatintl.com/usesapplications/infrastructure/infrastructure.shtml.

17. Digital Globe, 1/20/04, www.digitalglobe.com.

18. CIA, CIA Today.

19. Dilegge and Konynenberg, p. 175.

20. Verton, p. 74.

21. Denning, p. 167.

22. Ibid., p. 168.

23. Ibid., pp. 226–28.

24. Ibid., p. 228.

25. Ibid., p. 257.

26. Ibid., p. 258.

27. Verton, p. 28.

28. Ibid.

29. Ibid., p. 39.

30. Ibid., p. 49.

31. Dilegge, p. 175.

32. Kevin Poulson, "Zap!...And Your PC's Dead," *ZDNet News*, 9/9/99; 1/19/04, http://zdnet.com.com/2100-11-515644.html.

33. Robert Friedman, *Red Mafiya: How the Russian Mob Has Invaded America* (New York: Berkley Books, 2002), p. 210.

34. Rensselaer W. Lee III, "Transnational Organized Crime: An Overview," pp. 1–38, in *Transnational Crime in the Americas: An Interamerican Dialogue Book* (New York: Routledge, 1999), p. 13.

35. Francisco Thoumi, "The Impact of the Illegal Drug Industry on Columbia," in *Transnational Crime in the Americas: An Interamerican Dialogue Book* (New York: Routledge, 1999), p. 134.

36. Martin A. Gosch and Richard Hammer, *The Last Testament of Lucky Luciano* (Boston: Little, Brown and Co., 1975), p. 263.

Chapter 5: Funding, Procurement, and Training

1. Stephen Handelman, *Comrade Criminal: Russia's New Mafiya* (New London, CT: Yale University Press, 1995), p. 29.

2. Ibid., p. 221.

3. Ibid., p. 223.

4. Ibid., p. 236.

5. Ibid., p. 249.

6. Martin A. Gosch and Richard Hammer, *The Last Testament of Lucky Luciano* (Boston: Little, Brown and Co., 1975), p. 263.

7. Ibid., p. 277.

8. Martin Booth, *The Dragon Syndicates: The Global Phenomenon of the Triads* (New York: Carroll and Graft Publishing, Inc., 1999), p. 68.

9. Ibid., pp. 81–2.

10. Ibid., pp. 97–8.

11. Phil Williams and John Piccarelli, "Organized Crime in Ukraine: Challenge and Response," U.S. Department of Justice, Office of Justice Programs, date accessed 6/10/04, www.ojp.gov:80/nij/international/programs/challresponse.pdf, p. 13.

12. Testimony of John S. Pistole, Assistant Director, Counter-terrorism Division, FBI, before the House Committee on Financial Services Sub-Committee on Oversight Investigations, "Terrorist Financing Operations Section," 9/24/03; 6/10/04, www.fbi.gov//congress/congress03/pistole092403.htm, p. 4.

13. Ibid., p.5.

14. Douglas Farah, *Blood From Stones: The Secret Financial Network of Terror* (New York: Broadway Books, 2004), p. 140.

15. Testimony of Dennis M. Lorimel, Chief—Financial Crimes Section, FBI, before the House Committee on Financial Services, Subcommittee on Oversight and Investigations, 2/12/2002; 6/10/04, www.fbi.gov//congress/congress02/lorimel021202.htm, pp. 5–6.

16. Farah, p. 66.

17. Ibid., p. 19.

18. Ibid., p. 60.

19. Pistole, p. 3.

20. Ibid., p. 4.

21. Farah, p. 79.

22. Lorimel, p. 3.

23. U.S. Attorneys Office, "Terrorist Financing," 7/2003, Vol. 51, No. 4, U.S. Attorney's Bulletin; date accessed 6/6/04, www.usdoj.gov/usao/eousa/foia_reading_room/usab5104.pdf, p. 29.

24. Ibid., p. 24.

25. Farah, pp. 136–8.

26. Ibid., p. 155.

27. Pistole, p. 4.

28. Testimony of Steven C. McGraw, Assistant Director, Office of Intelligence, FBI, on international drug trafficking and terrorism before the Senate Judiciary Committee, Washington, DC, date accessed 8/27/03, www.fbi.gov/congress/congress03/mcgraw052003.htm, p. 1.

29. U.S. Department of Justice, DEA Resources—Drug Intelligence Brief—Drugs and Terrorism: A New Perspective, 9/2002; 6/10/04, www.usdoj.gov/dea/pubs/02039/02039p.html, p. 4.

30. Lorimel, p. 6.

31. Farah, pp. 146–47.

32. Lorimel, pp. 5–6.

33. U.S. Department of Treasury, "The Hawala Alternative Remittance System and Its Role in Money Laundering," prepared by the FINCEN in cooperation with Interpol/FOPAC, Patrick M. Jost and Harjit Singh Sandhu, date accessed 6/10/04, www.treasury.gov/offices/eotffc/key-issues/hawala/fincen-hawala.pdf, p. 5.

34. Ibid., p. 7.

35. Ibid., p. 8.

36. Ibid., p. 9.

37. Ibid., p. 10

38. Farah, p. 109.

39. Ibid., p. 114.

40. U.S. Department of State: Bureau of Politico-Military Affairs, Washington, DC, "Background Paper: The U.S. Approach to Combating the Spread of Small Arms," 6/2/01; date accessed 6/10/04, www.state.gov/t/pm/rls/fs/2001/3766pf.htm.

41. Robert I. Friedman; *Red Mafiya: How the Russian Mob Has Invaded America* (New York: Berkeley Books, 2002), p. 48.

42. Ibid., p. 99.

43. Ibid., p. 209.

44. Ibid., pp. 139–40.

45. Pete Abel, "Manufacturing Trends-Globalizing the Source," pp. 81–104, in *Running Guns: The Global Black Market in Small Arms* (London: Zed Books, Ltd., 2000), p. 82.

46. U.S. Department of State.

47. Handelman, p. 225.

48. Ibid., p. 236.

49. Williams and Piccarelli, p. 23.

50. Ibid., p. 25.

51. Farah, p. 45.

52. U.S. Department of State, pp. 1–2.

53. Lucy Mathiak and Lora Lumpe, "Government Gun Running to Guerrillas," in *Running Guns: The Global Black Market in Small Arms* (London: Zed Books, Ltd., 2000), p. 60.

54. Farah, pp. 37, 41–42.

55. U.S. Department of State, 7/2/01, p. 1.

56. Testimony of Marion E. (Spike) Bowman, Deputy General Counsel, FBI, before the Senate Select Committee on Intelligence, "Foreign Intelligence Surveillance Act," 7/31/02; date accessed 6/17/04, www.fbi.gov/congress/congress02/bowman073102.htm.

57. Martha Brill-Olcott and Bakhtiar Babajanov, "The Terrorist Notebooks," *Foreign Policy* 135 (March/April 2003), 32.

58. Ibid., p. 34.

59. Ibid., p. 35.

60. Ibid., p. 36.

61. U.S. Federal Bureau of Investigation; Congressional Statements, Special Agent Mary Deborah Doran, FBI, New York, before the September 11th, 2001, Commission, 6/16/04; date accessed 6/19/04, www.fbi.gov/congress/congress04/doran061604.htm.

Chapter 6: A Theory of Global Insurgency

1. Carl Von Clausewitz, *On War*, edited and translated by Michael Howard and Peter Paret (Princeton, NJ: Princeton University Press, 1976), p. 204.

2. Ibid., p. 481.

3. Ibid., p. 483.

4. Mao Zedong, *Mao Zedong on Guerrilla Warfare,* translated and intro-duction by B.G. Samuel B. Griffith, USMC (ret.) (New York: Praeger Publishing, 1967), p. 42.

5. Ibid., p. 43.

6. T. E. Lawrence, *Seven Pillars of Wisdom* (London: Penguin Books, 1926), p. 195.

7. Ibid., p. 197.

8. Ibid., p. 198.

9. Ibid., p. 201.

10. Ibid., p. 200.

11. Joseph S. Nye, Jr., *Soft Power: The Means to Success in World Politics* (New York: Public Affairs, 2004), p. 6.

12. Ibid., pp. 17, 91.

13. Malcolm Gladwell, *The Tipping Point: How Little Things Can Make a Big Difference* (Boston: Little, Brown and Co., 2002), p. 54.

14. Ibid., p. 203.

15. Ibid., p. 173.

16. Ibid., p. 70.

17. Charles Whiting, *Skorzeny: The Most Dangerous Man In Europe* (Conshohocken, PA: Combined Publishing, 1998), p. 116.

18. Charles Foley, *Commando Extraordinary* (New York: Bantam Books, 1989), p. 19.

19. Whiting, p. 64.

20. Ibid., p. 67.

21. Otto Skorzeny, *My Commando Operations* (Atglen, PA: Schiffer Publications, 1995), p. 164.

22. Ibid., p. 210.

23. Antonia Fraser, *Cromwell: The Lord Protector* (New York: Alfred A. Knopf, 1974), p. 92.

24. James D. Drake, *King Philip's War: Civil War in New England, 1675–1676* (Amherst, MA: University of Massachusetts Press, 1999), p. 79.

25. Ibid., p. 65.

26. Ibid., p. 78.

27. Ibid., p. 84.

28. Ibid., p. 125.

29. Ibid., p. 84.

30. Ibid., p. 86.

31. Ibid., p. 124.

32. Ibid., p. 119.

33. Ibid., pp. 131–154.

34. Ibid., pp. 156–7.

Chapter 7: Al Qaeda and HMS *Dreadnought*

1. Diana Preston, *The Boxer Rebellion* (New York: Berkley Books, 2000), p. x.

2. Ibid., p. 21.

3. Ibid., p. 52.

4. Ibid., pp. 59–60.

5. Ibid., p. 67.

6. Alex Abella and Scott Gordon, *Shadow Enemies* (Guilford CT: Lyons Press, 2002), p. 5.

7. Ibid., p. 21.

8. Ibid., p. 67.

9. Ibid., p. 22.

10. Rohan Gunaratna, *Inside Al Qaeda: Global Network of Terror* (New York: Berkley Books, 2002), p. 79.

11. Ibid., p. 80.

12. Ibid., p. 95.

13. Ibid., p. 105.

14. Ibid., pp. 151–54.

15. Osama Bin Laden, "Jihad Against Jews and Crusaders," in Walter Laqueur, ed., *Voices of Terror* (New York, Reed Press, 2004), pp. 410–12.

16. Sayed Qutb, "Jihad in the Cause of God," in Walter Laqueur, ed., *Voices of Terror* (New York: Reed Press, 2004), pp. 394–97.

17. Guneratna, p. 117.

18. Testimony of T. J. Caruso, Acting Assistant Director, Counter-terrorism Division, FBI, before the Subcommittee on Intelligence Operations and Terrorism, Committee on Foreign Relations, U.S. Senate, "Al Qaeda International," 12/18/04; www.fbi.gov//congress/congress01/caruso121801.htm.

19. Guneratna, p. 16.

20. Adolf Hitler, *Mein Kampf* (New York: Reynal and Hitchcock, 1940), p. 404.

21. Ibid., p. 405.

22. Ibid., p. 601.

23. Ibid., p. 845.

24. Ibid., p. 461.

25. Ibid., p. 237.

26. William L. Shirer, *The Rise and Fall of the Third Reich: A History of Nazi Germany* (New York; Simon and Schuster, 1960), p. 142.

27. Ibid., p. 159.

28. Ibid., p. 191.

29. Ibid., p. 201.

30. National Security Strategy of the United States of America, September 2002, pp. 13–16; date accessed 12/02, www.whitehouse.gov/nsc/nss.pdf

31. Russian General Staff, *The Soviet Afghan War: How a Superpower Fought and Lost,* translated and edited by Lester W. Grau and Michael A. Gress (Lawrence, KS: University of Kansas Press, 2002), p. 43.

32. Ibid., p. 19.

33. Ibid., p. 35.

34. Ibid., p. 26.

35. Ibid., p. 56.

36. Timothy L. Thomas, "The Battle For Grozny: Deadly Classroom for Urban Combat," *Parameters* (Summer 1999), 91.

37. Captain Chad A. Rupe, "The Battle for Grozny," *Armor* (May–June 1999), 22.

38. Joint Chiefs of Staff, FM 90-10 Manuevers on Urban Terrain, *Joint Electronic Library*, Approved Joint Publications, Selected Service Publications, Research Papers, Vol. 3, No. 1, May 1995, Developed by OC, Inc., for J-7 Joint Staff, p. 1-1.

39. Sun Tzu, *The Art of War*, edited and Forward by James Clavell (New York: Delacorte Press, 1983), p. 19.

Works Cited

Chapter 1: The Case for Global Insurgency

Bowden, Mark, *Blackhawk Down: A Story of Modern War*, New York, Atlantic Monthly Press, 1999.

Karnow, Stanley, *Vietnam: A History*, Middlesex, U.K.: Penguin Books, Ltd., 1983.

Mao Tze Tung, *On Guerrilla Warfare*, translated by Brigadier General Samuel B. Griffith, USMC (ret.), New York: Praeger Publishers, 1967.

Chapter 2: Leadership and Mobilization

Associated Press, "Concern Over Radical Relief Group," CNN, 01/06/05; 01/12/05, www.cnn.com/2005/WORLD/asiapcf/01/06/aceh.radicals/ap/index.html.

Boyd, Andrew, "Billionaires Crash the Extreme Costume Ball," pp. 152–60, in Mike Prokosch and Laura Raymonds, eds., *The Global Activists Manual*, New York: Thunder's Mouth Press/Nation Books, 2002.

CNN, "Purported bin Laden Tape Endorses Zarqawi," CNN, 12/27/04; 01/12/05, www.cnn.com/2004/WORLD/meast/12/27/binladen.tape/index.html.

Dolan, Mike, "The Indirect Action Network," pp. 228–29, in Mike Prokosch and Laura Raymonds, eds., *The Global Activists Manual*, New York: Thunder's Mouth Press/Nation Books, 2002.

Garrido, Maria, and Halavais, Alexander, "Mapping Networks of Support for the Zapatista Movement," pp. 165–84, in Martha McCaughey and Michael D. Ayers, eds., *Cyberactivism in Theory and Practice*, New York: Routledge, 2003.

Knapp, Don, and Associated Press, "Activists to WTO: Put People Over Profits," CNN, 11/29/99; 11/13/01, www.cnn.com/29/wto.seattle.02/index.html.

Lefevre, Greg, Barrett, Katharine, and Associated Press, "Seattle Mayor Declares Civil Emergency as WTO Unrest Grows," CNN, 11/30/99; 11/13/01 www.cnn.com/us/9911/30/wto.03/index.html.

Maxwell, Mary Beth, "Coalition Building: Lessons From the Jobs With Justice Model," pp. 72–77, in Mike Prokosch and Laura Raymonds, eds., *The Global Activists Manual*, New York: Thunder's Mouth Press/Nation Books, 2002.

McCaughey, Martha, and Ayers, Michael D., eds., *Cyberactivism in Theory and Practice*, New York: Routledge, 2003.

Prokosch, Mike, and Raymond, Laura, eds., *The Global Activists Manual*, New York: Thunder's Mouth Press/Nation Books, 2002.

Rheingold, Howard, *Smartmobs: The Next Social Revolution*, Cambridge, MA: Perseus Publishing, 2003.

Ronfeldt, David, Arquilla, John, Fuller, Graham E., and Fuller, Melissa, *The Zapatista Social Netwar in Mexico*, Santa Barbara, CA: RAND, 1998.

Starhawk, "How We Really Shut Down the WTO," pp. 134–39, in Mike Prokosch and Laura Raymond, eds., *The Global Activists Manual*, New York: Thunder's Mouth Press/Nation Books, 2002.

Stephan, Martin, "The Fight Against Boise Cascade," pp. 26–31, in Mike Prokosch and Laura Raymond, eds., *The Global Activists Manual*, New York: Thunder's Mouth Press/Nation Books, 2002.

United Nations, DPINGO Section, 8/28/03, www.un.org/dpi/ngosection/asp/form.asp.

Williams, Phil, "Transnational Criminal Organizations: Strategic Alliances," *The Washington Quarterly* (Winter 1995) CSIS/MIT, 1994, pp. 57–72.

Chapter 3: Global Insurgency Warfare

Asprey, Robert B., *War in the Shadows: The Guerrilla in History*, Vol. 1, New York: Doubleday and Co., 1974.

Collins, John M., *Military Geography for Professionals and the Public*, Washington, DC: Brasseys, 1998.

Ronfeldt, David, Arquilla, John, Fuller, Graham E., and Fuller, Melissa, *The Zapatista Social Netwar in Mexico*, Santa Barbara, CA: RAND, 1998.

Thomas, Timothy L., "The Battle for Grozny: Deadly Classroom for Urban Combat," *Parameters* (Summer 1999), 50–58.

U.S. Department of State, "Patterns of Global Terrorism, Appendix B: Background Information on Designated Foreign Terrorist Organizations," 04/30/03; 08/28/03, http://www.state.gov/s/ct/rls/pgtrpt/2002/html/1999/pf.htm.

Chapter 4: Intelligence

Academy for Competitive Intelligence, 1/20/04, www.academyci.com/about.
Aero Bureau Corp., "News From Above," 1/20/04, www.Aerobureau.com.

Bunker, Robert J., ed., *Non-state Threats and Future Wars*, London: Frank Cass and Co., Ltd., 2003.

CIA Factbook on Intelligence 2002: The Intelligence Cycle, 12/10/03, www.odci.gov/cia/publications/factell/intelligence_cycle.html.

CIA Today—Different Kinds of Intelligence, 12/21/03, www.odci.gov/cia/publication/cia_today/ciatoday_06.shtml.

Denning, Dorothy E., *Information Warfare and Security*, Reading, MA: Addison Wesley Longman, Inc., 1999.

Dilegge, David P., and Van Konynenberg, Mathew, "The Chechens and Urban Operations: View From the Wolves Den," pp. 171–84, in Robert J. Bunker, ed., *Non-state Threats and Future Wars*, London: Frank Cass and Co., Ltd., 2003.

Digital Globe, 1/20/04, www.digitalglobe.com.

Farer, Tom, "Conclusion—Fighting Transnational Organized Crime: Measures Short of War," pp. 245–96, in Tom Farer, ed., *Transnational Crime in the Americas: An Interamerican Dialogue Book,* New York: Routledge, 1999.

Farer, Tom, ed. *Transnational Crime in the Americas: An Interamerican Dialogue Book,* New York: Routledge, 1999.

Friedman, Robert, *Red Mafiya: How the Russian Mob Has Invaded America,* New York: Berkley Books, 2002.

Goldstein, Emanuel, *2600: The Hacker Quarterly*, St. James, NY: 2600 Enterprises, Fall 2003, vol. 23, no.3.

Gosch, Martin A., and Hammer, Richard, *The Last Testament of Lucky Luciano,* Boston: Little, Brown and Co., 1975.

Grewe, Barbara, Jacobson, Michael, Eldridge, Thomas, and Ginsberg, Susan, "Staff Statement No. 10—Threats and Responses in 2001," pp. 272–92, in Steven Strasser, ed., *The 9/11 Investigations*, New York: Public Affairs Reports, 2004.

ImageSat International, 1/20/04, www.imagesatintl.com.

ImageSat International, About Us, 1/20/04, www.imagesatintl.com/aboutus/aboutus.shtml.

ImageSat International, Infrastructure, 1/20/04, www.imagesatintl.com/usesapplications/infrastructure/infrastructure.shtml.

ImageSat International, National Security, 1/20/04, www.imagesatintl.com/usesapplications/nationalsecurity/security.shtml.

Lee, Rensselaer W., III, "Transnational Organized Crime: An Overview," pp. 1–38, in Tom Farer, ed., *Transnational Crime in the Americas: An Interamerican Dialogue Book*, New York: Routledge, 1999.

Mitnick, Kevin, and Simon, William L., *The Art of Deception*, Indianapolis, IN: Wiley Publishing, 2002.

Poulson, Kevin, "Zap!...and Your PC's Dead," *ZDNet News*, 9/9/99; 1/19/04, http://zdnet.com.com/2100-11-515644.html.

Riskworld, 1/20/04, www.riskworld.com/websites/webfiles/ws5aa013.htm.

Space Imaging, 1/20/04, www.spaceimaging.com/corporate/default.htm.

Steven Strasser, ed., *The 9/11 Investigations*, New York: Public Affairs Reports, 2004.

Sullivan, John P., and Bunker, Robert J., "Drug Cartels, Street Gangs, and Warlords," pp. 40–53, in Robert J. Bunker, ed., *Non-state Threats and Future Wars*, London: Frank Cass and Co., Ltd, 2003.

Thoumi, Francisco, "The Impact of the Illegal Drug Industry on Columbia," pp. 117–42, in Tom Farer, ed., *Transnational Crime in the Americas: An Interamerican Dialogue Book,* New York: Routledge, 1999.

Verton, Dan, *Black Ice: The Invisible Threat of Cyberterrorism*, Emeryville, CA, McGraw-Hill, 2003.

Chapter 5: Funding, Procurement, and Training

Abel, Pete, "Manufacturing Trends—Globalizing the Source," pp. 81–104, in Lora Lumpe, ed., *Running Guns: The Global Black Market in Small Arms,* London: Zed Books, Ltd., 2000.

Booth, Martin, *The Dragon Syndicates: The Global Phenomenon of the Triads,* New York: Carroll and Graft Publishing, Inc., 1999.

Brill-Olcott, Martha, and Babajanov, Bakhtiar, "The Terrorist Notebooks," *Foreign Policy* 135 (March/April 2003), 30–40.

Farah, Douglas, *Blood From Stones: The Secret Financial Network of Terror,* New York: Broadway Books, 2004.

Friedman, Robert I., *Red Mafiya: How the Russian Mob Has Invaded America,* New York: Berkeley Books, 2002.

Gosch, Martin A., and Hammer, Richard, *The Last Testament of Lucky Luciano,* Boston: Little Brown and Co., 1975.

Handelman, Stephen, *Comrade Criminal: Russia's New Mafiya*, New London, CT: Yale University Press, 1995.

Lumpe, Lora, ed., *Running Guns: The Global Black Market in Small Arms,* London: Zed Books, Ltd., 2000.

Mathiak, Lucy, and Lumpe, Lora, "Government Gun Running to Guerrillas," pp. 55–80, in Lora Lumpe, ed., *Running Guns: The Global Black Market in Small Arms,* London: Zed Books, Ltd., 2000.

Testimony of Marion E. (Spike) Bowman, Deputy General Counsel, FBI, before the Senate Select Committee on Intelligence, July 31, 2002, "Foreign Intelligence Surveillance Act," 6/17/04, www.fbi.gov/congress/congress02/bowman073102.htm.

Testimony of Dennis M. Lorimel, Chief—Financial Crimes Section, FBI, before the House Committee on Financial Services, Subcommittee on Oversight and Investigations, 2/12/02; date accessed 6/10/04, www.fbi.gov//congress/congress02/lorimel021202.htm.

Testimony of Steven C. McGraw, Assistant Director, Office of Intelligence, FBI, on International Drug Trafficking and Terrorism before the Senate Judiciary Committee, Washington, DC, www.fbi.gov/congress/congress03/mcgraw052003.htm.

Testimony of John S. Pistole, Assistant Director, Counter-terrorism Division, FBI, before the House Committee on Financial Services Sub-Committee on

Oversight Investigations, "Terrorist Financing Operations Section," 9/24/03; 6/10/04, www.fbi.gov//congress/congress03/pistole101403.htm.

U.S. Attorneys Office, "Terrorist Financing," July 2003, Vol. 51, No. 4, U.S. Attorney's Bulletin; 6/6/04, www.usdoj.gov/usao/eousa/foia_reading_room/usab5104.pdf.

U.S. Department of Justice, DEA Resources—Drug Intelligence Brief—Drugs and Terrorism: A New Perspective, 9/02; date accessed 6/10/04, www.usdoj.gov/dea/pubs/02039/02039p.html.

U.S. Department of State: Bureau of Politico-Military Affairs, Washington, DC, "Background Paper: The U.S. Approach to Combating the Spread of Small Arms," 6/2/01; date accessed 6/10/04, www.state.gov/t/pm/rls/fs/2001/3766pf.htm.

U.S. Department of Treasury, "The Hawala Alternative Remittance System and Its Role in Money Laundering," prepared by the FINCEN in cooperation with Interpol/FOPAC, Patrick M. Jost and Harjit Singh Sandhu, www.treasury.gov/offices/eotffc/key-issues/hawala/fincen-hawala.pdf.

U.S. Federal Bureau of Investigation; Congressional Statements, Special Agent Mary Deborah Doran, FBI, New York, before the September 11, 2001, Commission, 6/16/04; date accessed 6/19/04, www.fbi.gov/congress/congress04/doran061604.htm.

Williams, Phil, and Piccarelli, John, "Organized Crime in Ukraine: Challenge and Response," U.S. Department of Justice, Office of Justice Programs, date accessed 6/10/04, www.ojp.gov:80/nij/international/programs/challresponse.pdf.

Chapter 6: A Theory of Global Insurgency

Clausewitz, Carl von, *On War*, edited and translated by Michael Howard and Peter Paret, Princeton, NJ: Princeton University Press, 1976.

Drake, James D., *King Philip's War: Civil War in New England, 1675–1676*, Amherst, MA: University of Massachusetts Press, 1999.

Foley, Charles, *Commando Extraordinary*, New York: Bantam Books, 1989.

Fraser, Antonia, *Cromwell: The Lord Protector*, New York: Alfred A. Knopf, 1974.

Gladwell, Malcolm, *The Tipping Point: How Little Things Can Make a Big Difference*, Boston: Little, Brown and Co., 2002.

Lawrence, T. E., *Seven Pillars of Wisdom*, London: Penguin Books, 1926.

Mao Zedong, *Mao Zedong on Guerrilla Warfare*, translated and introduction by BG Samuel B. Griffith, USMC (ret.), New York: Praeger Publishing, 1967.

Nye, Joseph S., Jr., *Soft Power: The Means to Success in World Politics*, New York: Public Affairs, 2004.

Schoenbrun, David, *Soldiers of the Night: The Story of the French Resistance*, New York: Meridian Books, 1980.

Skorzeny, Otto, *My Commando Operations*, Atglen, PA: Schiffer Publications, 1995.

Whiting, Charles, *Skorzeny: The Most Dangerous Man in Europe*, Conshohocken, PA: Combined Publishing, 1998.

Chapter 7: Al Qaeda and HMS *Dreadnought*

Abella, Alex, and Gordon, Scott, *Shadow Enemies,* Guilford, CT: Lyons Press, 2002.

Gunaratna, Rohan, *Inside Al Qaeda: Global Network of Terror,* New York: Berkley Books, 2002.

Hitler, Adolf, *Mein Kampf,* New York: Reynal and Hitchcock, 1940.

Joint Chiefs of Staff, FM 90-10 Manuevers on Urban Terrain, *Joint Electronic Library*, Approved Joint Publications, Selected Service Publications, Research Papers, Vol. 3, No. 1, May 1995, Developed by OC, Inc., for J-7 Joint Staff.

Bin Laden, Osama, "Jihad Against Jews and Crusaders," in Walter Laqueur, ed., *Voices of Terror,* New York: Reed Press, 2004.

Laqueur, Walter, ed., *Voices of Terror,* New York: Reed Press, 2004.

Preston, Diana, *The Boxer Rebellion,* New York: Berkley Books, 2000.

Qutb, Sayid, "Jihad in the Cause of God," in Walter Laqueur, ed., *Voices of Terror,* New York: Reed Press, 2004.

Rupe, Captain Chad A., "The Battle for Grozny," *Armor* (May–June 1999).

Russian General Staff, *The Soviet Afghan War: How a Superpower Fought and Lost,* translated and edited by Lester W. Grau and Michael A. Gress, Lawrence, KS: University of Kansas Press, 2002.

Shirer, William L., *The Rise and Fall of the Third Reich: A History of Nazi Germany,* New York: Simon and Schuster, 1960.

Sun Tzu, *The Art of War,* edited and Forward by James Clavell, New York: Delacorte Press, 1983.

Testimony of T. J. Caruso, Acting Assistant Director, Counter-terrorism Division, FBI, before the Subcommittee on Intelligence Operations and Terrorism, Committee on Foreign Relations, U.S. Senate, "Al Qaeda International," 12/18/01; www.fbi.gov//congress/congress01/caruso121801.htm.

Thomas, Timothy L., "The Battle for Grozny: Deadly Classroom for Urban Combat," *Parameters* (Summer 1999), 50–58.

U.S. National Security Council, *The National Security Strategy of the United States of America,* 1/10/03, www.whitehouse.gov/nsc/nss.pdf.

Works Consulted

Anderson, Jon Lee, *Guerrillas: Journeys in the Insurgent World*, New York: Penguin Books, 2004.

Arquilla, John, and Ronfeldt, David, *In Athena's Camp: Preparing for Conflict in the Information Age*, Santa Monica, CA: RAND, 1997.

Bergin, Peter L., *Holy War Inc.: Inside the Secret World of Osama bin Laden*, New York: Touchstone Press, 2002.

Century Foundation, *Defeating the Jihadists: A Blueprint for Action*, chaired by Richard Clarke, New York: Century Foundation Press, 2004.

Chaliand, Gerard, *Guerrilla Strategies: An Historical Anthology From the Long March to Afghanistan*, Berkeley, CA: University of California Press, 1982.

Cockburn, Alexander, and St. Clair, Jeffrey, *Five Days That Shook the World: Seattle and Beyond*, London: Verso Press, 2000.

Coll, Steve, *Ghost Wars: The Secret History of the CIA, Afghanistan, and bin Laden From the Soviet Invasion to September 11th, 2001*, New York: Penguin Press, 2004.

Emerson, Steven, *American Jihad: The Terrorists Living Among Us*, New York: Free Press, 2002.

Gall, Carlotta, and De Waal Thomas, *Chechnya: Calamity in the Caucasus*, New York: New York University Press, 1998.

Goltz, Thomas, *Chechnya Diary: A War Correspondent's Story of Surviving the War in Chechnya*, New York: Thomas Dunne Books, 2003.

Hammes, Col. Thomas X., USMC, *The Sling and The Stone: On War in the 21st Century*, St. Paul, MN: Zenith Press, 2004.

Holloway, John, and Pezael, Eloina, *Zapatista! Reinventing Revolution in Mexico*, London: Pluto Press, 1998.

Howard, Russell D., and Sawyer, Capt. Reid L., *Terrorism and Counterterrorism: Understanding the New Security Environment—Readings and Interpretations*, Guilford, NY: McGraw-Hill, 2003.

Lawrence, T. E., *Revolt in the Desert*, Tess Press, 1926.

Mackinlay, John, *Globalism and Insurgency*, Adelphi Paper 352, International Institute for Strategic Studies, Oxford, U.K.: Oxford University Press, 2002.

Schilling, William R., *Nontraditional Warfare: 21st Century Threats and Responses*, London: Brasseys UK, 2002.

Schultz, Duane, *Quantrill's War: The Life and Times of William Clarke Quantrill*, New York: St. Martins Griffin, 1996.

Ullman, Harlan K., *Finishing Business: Ten Steps to Defeat Global Terror*, Annapolis, MD: Naval Institute Press, 2004.

Van Creveld, Martin, *The Transformation of War*, New York: Free Press, 1991.

Index

Access, 14–16, 130; egalitarianism and, 131; to power, 14–16. *See also specific topics*
Activation, 43–46
Adaptability, 21–23
Aerobureau, 84
Afghanistan, 11, 102, 139, 153
AFL-CIO (American Federation of Labor and Congress of Industrial Organizations), 31
Agenda, 23–26, 116
Aidid, General, 7–9
AK-47, 107
Al Qaeda, 141, 145; bridging communities, 57; changing the world, 141, 154; charities and, 100; connections/network, 57, 145–48; coordinating action in multiple places, 146–47; as dark side of global political activism, 34; defeating, 54, 154–55; diamonds and, 99; funding, 99–101; generates services like governments to fight wars, 145; as global movement, 6, 145–48; importance, 57; issue motivating, 146, 147; as religious group, 56, 146; rise of Nazis compared with rise of, 149–51; seeking popular support, 145; taking action in multiple places, 147; tested,

145–48; uses all available tools, 147–48; as worldwide, 145–46
"Amateur soldiers," ix, x, 129–30; beating professional soldiers, 129–30
Ambushes, 10, 57, 128
American Civil War, 51
American Federation of Labor and Congress of Industrial Organizations (AFL-CIO), 31
Atomic bomb, 15, 106
Attacks: location, 20 (*see also* Battlefields); timing, 20, 127
Attrition, 60

Banks, 98–102
Battlefields, new, 62–66
Benevolence International Foundation, 97
Bin Laden, Osama, 73, 146
Bombing, 104; conventional, 57–58; suicide, 57
Bombs, making, 104
Boxer Rebellion, 141–44
British, 73, 123. *See also* King Philip's War

Camouflage, 10, 63–64
Cell phones, 43–44, 86
Central Intelligence Agency (CIA), 72, 78, 84

Change, 14–16; need for, 155–59
Charities, funding from, 96–97, 100
Chechnya, 52, 93–94; independence,
  6, 56; insurgents and, 6, 153;
  intelligence, 81, 85, 90;
  wars in, 6, 81
Chiang Kai-shek, 94, 95
Chiapas, 52; implications, 29–30;
  uprising, 28–29
Chinese, 30, 94–95, 141–43.
  See also Mao Tse-tung
Cities: fighting in, 153–54; reasons
  for operating in, 63–67, 107–8
Citizens Trade Commission
  (CTC), 36
City Hall, 15–16
Clausewitz, Karl von, 124
Coast watchers, 70, 73
Cold War, 16, 151
Cole, U.S.S., 70, 147
Committee-based organizations,
  38–39, 44
Communications, 7, 27.
  See also Activation
Communism, 18; fall of, 16–18, 30,
  103, 148–49, 152. *See also* Cold
  War; Vietnam War
Concentration, 50–54. *See also*
  Dispersal/dispersion
Connections, 36, 122. *See also* Issue
  constellations; Networks and
  partnerships
Conventional war, 138; contrasted
  with unconventional war, 115–17;
  evolution, 152; uniformity, 62
Counterfeiting, 89–90
Counterinsurgency orientation, 155
Creativity, 21–23
Criminal operations: for fundraising,
  100. *See also* Organized crime;
  Transnational criminal
  organizations
Cromwell, Oliver, 130
Cruise missiles, 61
Currency, 98–99

Development, NGOs oriented to, 36
Digital Globe, 84
Disarmament, NGOs oriented to, 36
Dispersal/dispersion, 50–54,
  61–62, 121

Diversity, 158
Drug trade, 30–31

Earth Justice Legal Defense Fund, 32
Earth Liberation Front, 56
Eclecticism, 33, 41, 50–54
Education. *See* Training
Environmental groups, 36, 56
EZLN, 28, 29, 40, 52

Factions, working together.
  See Connections; Group
  connections; Networks and
  partnerships
False information, 90
Finances, 61, 64, 123. *See also*
  Funding
French Resistance, 52–54, 120
Fuld, Leonard, 78
Funding (and fundraising), 61,
  96–103; changes in, 116;
  illegitimate, 96–100; insurgent,
  97–98; legitimate, 96–98;
  permanent, 97–98;
  semi-permanent, 97, 98
Funding fronts, 96–97

Germany, 126, 127, 149–51. *See also*
  Nazis; World War II
Gladwell, Malcolm, 128
Global Exchange, 32
Global insurgency(ies), 2; changes
  necessary to defeat, 137–40;
  contrasted with conventional
  warfare, 115–17; defining the
  adversary when fighting, 55–57,
  138; global reach, 67; how long
  they will be a threat, 133–34;
  implications, 137–40; and
  importance of context, 18–23;
  limits, 125–26; model of, 117–18;
  possibility of being defeated by,
  122–23; power, 116, 152; template,
  118–19; *vs.* terrorism, 123–24;
  three factors for success, 14–18;
  understanding, 115–19; what
  is happening, 4–8. *See also*
  Insurgency; *specific topics*
Globalism, 37–38, 95, 130, 131
Global support, 128
Gold, 99, 101

Governmental authority, 23–24
Grassroots movements, 35
Group connections: importance, 36, 121–22. *See also* Issue constellations; Networks and partnerships
Grozny, 153
Guerrillas, 63. *See also* Chechnya; Mao; Tamil Tigers; Viet Cong
Gulf War, 152, 153; as conventional war, 138, 152; new paradigm, 152; as response model, 138
Gunpowder, 132

Hacking, 89, 90
HAMAS, 56, 96–97, 99, 101
Hawala, 101–2
Hezbollah, 99
Hierarchical authority, 39
Hierarchy, 38–40, 42, 45, 52–53; *vs.* committee, 38–39
High-energy radio frequency (HERF) guns, 90
Historical parallels that shed light on what to do, 134–36, 149–51
Hitler, Adolf, 126, 127, 149
Holy Land Foundation for Relief and Development, 99–100
Homeland security, 157
"Hub and nodes," 44
Human rights, NGOs oriented to, 36
HUMINT (human intelligence), 70, 71, 73, 79–82

Imagesat International, 84
IMINT (imagery intelligence), 82–85
India, 37
Indonesia, 34, 58
Information, false, 90
Information technology, 7, 17, 132; activation and, 43–46
Infrastructure: conventional war dependence on, 120; floating, 102; funding, 102; physical, 102
Insurgency: differences with governments, 18–21; effectiveness, ix, 5, 119–20, 124–25, 128–30, 152, 153; fragility, 126; local knowledge, 9–10; principles, 54; reasons for, 8–14; what we can do about, 155–59; why it creates such

problems for conventional foes, 120–21. *See also specific topics*
Insurgent groups, classification of, 56
Insurgents: advantages, 9–14, 23, 29–30, 34, 53, 59–62 (*see also specific advantages*); amateur, ix, x, 129–30; taking over a country: 126–127
Intelligence, 26, 69–75, 92; amateur, 74–75; analysis and production, 71, 87–88; changes in, 116; collection, 70–71, 76–87; connecting the dots, 87–88; consumer, 71–72; decision makers and, 73, 87; direction and planning, 75–76; dissemination, 88–89; government, 69, 71; imagery, 82–85; importance to war, 69–70; native, 65; sabotage, 89–91; signal, 85–87; types, 76. *See also* HUMINT; Insurgency, local knowledge; Knowledge; Organized crime; OSINT
Internet, 43, 71, 86, 88–89, 108
Iraq: U.S. invasion of, 9; U.S. occupation of, 58, 60
Islam, 146. *See also* Al Qaeda; *specific topics*
Islamic Resistance Movement. *See* HAMAS
Issue constellations, 3, 39–40, 47
Issue organizations/groups, 4–5, 91; advantages over governments, 5, 20, 23; collaboration, 40–41; defined, 3; effectiveness, 5, 9, 46; "flat organization," 9; goals, 13, 40
Issues: have always been around, 132–33; and their characteristics, 35–38; unaddressed, 35

Jewels, 99, 101
Johnson, Lyndon B., 23

Kidnapping, 57, 58, 129
King Philip's War, 134–36
Knowledge, 25; local, 9–10. *See also* Intelligence
Kurdish Workers Party (PKK), 100

Lawrence, T. E. (Lawrence of Arabia), 124–25

Leadership, 24, 26, 41–43
Libyan model, 139
Local knowledge, 9–10
Location of attacks, 20. *See also*
  Battlefields
Longshoremen Union, 32
Luciano, Lucky, 91, 94

Mao Tse-tung, 13, 14, 124
Maquis, 52
Marcos, Subcommandante, 29
Message, crafting a, 42
Mexico, 28–30
Middle East: insurgent operations,
  58. *See also specific topics*
Mob. *See* Organized crime
Mogadishu, 153
Money, 98–101. *See also* Finances;
  Funding
Money laundering, 31
Moscow opera house, 6
Moveon.org, 34
Muslim Brotherhood, 101

Nationalism, 126, 127
Native intelligence, 65
Nazis, 94, 126, 127, 149–51;
  American, 141, 143–44
Networks and partnerships, 27–28,
  30–35, 56–57; *vs.* hierarchies,
  38–39. *See also* Connections; Group
  connections; Issue constellations
Nigerians, 30–31
9/11. *See* September 11, 2001
Nongovernmental organizations
  (NGOs), 3, 31–36; Chiapas and, 28,
  29; eclectic, 33; front, 97; Islamic,
  97; issues, 35–36; joint ventures,
  28–29, 31–33
Normandy invasion in World War II,
  52, 95, 144
North American Free Trade
  Agreement (NAFTA), 36
Nuclear weapons, 15, 106
Nye, Joseph, 127–28

Office of Naval Intelligence, 91
Oklahoma City bombing, 104
Openness, 16–17, 130–32
Open Source Solutions, 78
Operations, 57–62

Organization, 14, 38–41
Organized crime, 58, 91–95, 104,
  106, 107
OSINT (open source intelligence),
  77–79

Pakistan, 102
Palestine Liberation Organization
  (PLO), 50
Palestinians, 56. *See also* HAMAS
Peace: NGOs oriented to, 36;
  possibilities for, 137
Philip, King, 134–36
Philippines, 58
Political agendas, unplanned,
  148–51
Popular support, 122, 126, 145,
  154, 156
Portfolio approach, 50–54
Power, 116, 152; access to, 14–16;
  "soft," 127
Precision-guided munitions,
  152, 153
Procurement, 25, 103–8
Protests, global, 7, 31–33

Qaeda, Al. *See* Al Qaeda

Religious groups, 36, 56, 142. *See also
  specific groups*
Resilience, 130, 148
Resolution *vs.* reward motivation,
  40, 41
Resources, gathering, 116
Royal Observer Corps, 73
Rural areas, 64
Russia, 81, 91, 153

SAAR Foundation, 100
Sabotage, 89–91
Satellites, 83, 85
Seattle, 7, 31, 38–40
Security, 36, 157; imbalance between
  wealth production and, 156
Separatist movements, 56
September 11, 2001, 1, 11–13, 57, 61,
  72, 113–14, 147
Shinrikyo, Aum, 105
Sierra Club, 32
SIGINT (signal intelligence), 85–87
Skorzeny, Otto, 129

Smuggling, 106
Social engineering, 81–82. *See also* HUMINT
"Soft power," 127
Somalia, 7–8, 153
Soviet Afghan war, 153
Space Imaging, 84
Sri Lanka, 90
Standard operating procedures (SOPs), 10
Submarines, 61
Suicide bombings, 57
Sun Tzu, 157
Support: active *vs.* passive, 42; global, 128; popular, 122, 126, 145, 154, 156
Synchronization of effort, 44

Tainted finding, 96
Taliban, 11, 54
Tamil Tigers, 56, 90
Targets, 59–60
TCOs. *See* Transnational criminal organizations
Teamsters, 32, 36
Technology, 1–2, 19, 152; access to, 17; facilitates connections, 17–18; intelligence, 85–86; uselessness, 8–9, 67. *See also* Communications; Information technology
Terrorism, 5, 8, 11, 139; definitions, 123; as a label, 123–24; war on, 1, 34, 54. *See also* September 11, 2001
Tet Offensive, 22–23
Text messaging, 43–44
Training, 25, 108–13; education, 108–11; practice, 108–9
Training camps, 110, 111
Transnational criminal organizations (TCOs), 6–7, 30–32, 106, 107; linkages/partnerships, 30–32
Triads, 94–95
Turkey, 125

Unconventional war: in cities, 153–54; evolution, 152
United for a Fair Economy, 32
Uranium, 106
Urban areas. *See* Cities

Viet Cong, 22–23
Vietnam War, 22–23
Violence: changes in, 116; directly serving politics, 127; political goals and, 156

Warfare, 49–50, 153; changing, 5–8, 55; dispersal and eclecticism, 50–54 (*see also* Dispersal/dispersion); a new path for, 151–55; redefined, 66–67. *See also specific topics*
War(s): future possibilities for, 137; recent changes in, 1; replaced by bloodless conflict, 127–28; winning, 124–25; winning battles but losing the, ix–x, 122, 123, 130. *See also specific topics*
Weapons, 104–5; buying, 103; in cities, 66, 107–8; materials for, 106; precision-guided, 152, 153; small arms, 104–5, 107; TCOs and, 106, 107; trafficking, 104, 106–7; transfers, 106–7. *See also* Procurement
Weapons of mass destruction (WMD), 95, 105–6
World Trade Center, 61. *See also* September 11, 2001
World Trade Organization (WTO), 31–33
World War I, 123
World War II, 52–54, 73, 94, 95, 120, 129, 143–44

Yemen, 70

Zapatista National Liberation Army (EZLN), 28, 29, 40, 52

About the Author

MICHAEL C. FOWLER is a defense analyst and freelance consultant, concentrating on topics such as insurgency, the evolution of war, and homeland security. He teaches at Roger Williams University in Rhode Island.